2

Date Due

Monday, 21st October 1805, saw the greatest naval battle the world had ever known. Eight miles off Cape Trafalgar on the southern coast of Portugal, in rough seas, the combined French and Spanish fleets of Admiral Villeneuve clashed with the English fleet, commanded by Admiral Lord Nelson from his flagship, the *Victory*. Villeneuve's fleet included the *Trinidada*, the largest warship afloat. But Nelson's smaller fleet had superior morale and training, and, with the use of a dangerous and brilliant tactic, inflicted a crushing defeat. "Half a victory would but half content me," Nelson had said. Of 33 enemy battleships 15 were sunk, blew up or ran ashore, 8 were taken as prizes, and only 10 limped back, with shattered masts and hulls, to Cadiz. Never before had England celebrated such a naval triumph. Gone were Napoleon's dreams of blockading England, and of ferrying a massive invasion force across the Channel. But as the bells of St. Paul's Cathedral rang their victory peal, men wept at the death of the hero of Trafalgar, shot by a musket ball in the shoulder while directing the battle.

Roger Hart uses a treasury of documents – memoirs, ships' logs, Admiralty reports, private papers – to piece together Nelson's remarkable victory, and to portray seafaring life in a navy notorious for its press gangs, its flogging officers, and its grim life below decks.

Frontispiece On the deck of H.M.S. *Victory* at the height of the Battle of
Trafalgar, 1805

England Expects

Roger Hart

*"Half a victory would but half
content me." – Admiral Lord
Nelson, 6th September, 1805.*

WAYLAND PUBLISHERS · LONDON
G. P. PUTNAM'S SONS · NEW YORK

In this series

Copyright © 1972 by Wayland (Publishers) Ltd.
101 Grays Inn Road, London WC1
All rights reserved. This book, or parts there of, must not be
reproduced in any form without permission.

SBN: (England): 85340 162 4
SBN: (United States): 399-11051-8
Library of Congress Catalogue Card Number: 72-87617

Printed in England by The Garden City Press Ltd.
Letchworth, Hertfordshire SG6 1JS

Contents

The Illustrations

1 The Struggle for Seapower

AS AN ISLAND, Britain's security depended on control of the sea.
Only thus could she stop an invader crossing to her shores. For
many centuries, Britain had waged wars with France. With the
outbreak of the French Revolution in 1789, and the subsequent
rise of Napoleon, England's shores were once again in danger. In
1805, the year of Trafalgar, Napoleon dreamed of sending a great
army across the Channel from Boulogne to invade England.
Seapower became ever more vital for England's safety.

Seapower

A major task of the fleet was to try and blockade all the main
European ports where the French and allied Spanish navies were
based. The main ones were Brest, Boulogne and Flushing on the
Channel coast; Rochefort on the French coast; Ferrol, Vigo and
Cadiz on the Spanish and Portuguese coasts; and Toulon in the
Mediterranean (see map page 12). The Admiralty had to stop
Napoleon making a "grand junction" of all his naval squadrons,
and forming one great battle fleet strong enough to drive Britain's
ships out of the narrow Channel straits. One day, Britain hoped to
be able to destroy Napoleon's seapower in a decisive naval battle.
This could happen only when the navy had enough sound ships, and
when a good number of French and Spanish ships could be lured
out of their bases, and into battle. To do all this, the British fleet
was organized into two main squadrons, one in the Channel, and
the other in the Mediterranean under Admiral Lord Nelson.

*Blockading
Napoleon*

The war with France before 1805 had shown weaknesses in the
state of Britain's battleships. But the Admiralty now made rapid
progress in building up the fleet. Old vessels were refitted, new ones
were laid down. Ships' stores were ordered. Sir Charles Middleton,

*Building a
fleet*

Opposite Hoisting troops and horses aboard an English battleship

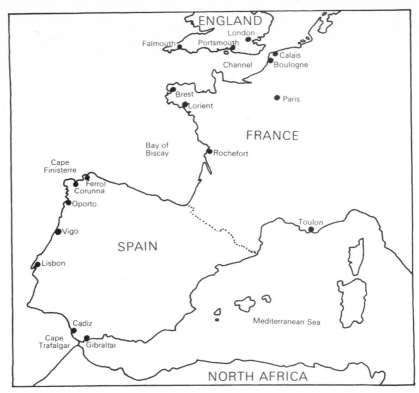

Map showing the main British, French and Spanish naval bases during the Napoleonic wars

appointed First Lord of the Admiralty in May, 1804, wrote: "The first thing, therefore, was to take in hand, immediately, all the ships that were in want of small repair. We were by this time strong in the number and quality of our shipwrights and caulkers. The stores were greatly increased, and all our storehouses arranged with separate berths for every ship's stores . . . Instead of having all the storehouses looked over for single ship's stores, every ship had the power of carrying off her own in 24 hours, instead of weeks, according to the old custom . . .

"The advantages arising from these preparations are incredible in the hands of an active administration. The having so many ships prepared for sea, and everything else that belonged to them, ready; the having coppered transports of our own instead of waiting for hired ones; and upwards of £3,000,000 in necessary stores in our arsenals, gave such advantages that the fleet, in my successor's time, was fitted out with a rapidity never known before . . . (1)"

12

Admiral Nelson's flagship, H.M.S. *Victory*, at anchor

The British fleet was still short of ships, but it was in far better shape than the French. A naval historian wrote: "The outbreak of the French Revolution reduced the French navy to chaos. For many of the brilliant professional officers there was left no choice between exile and the scaffold. It seemed that the very efficiency which dated from the institutions of pre-revolutionary France was itself a crime in 1789. Loud-voiced sentiments of liberty and patriotism now did duty for the discipline and training . . .

"Good gunnery and seamanship disappeared with the trained men. The manning of the ships was a perpetual problem. The condition of the men on board was very miserable, and the ships themselves were ill-found and short of spare sails and rigging. Napoleon was powerless, at short notice, to galvanise his navy into life and vigour, though he often refused to accept the doleful reports of his subordinates (2)."

Indeed, "Between 1793 and 1800 the condition of the French

The French fleet

13

fleet was such that the danger of serious invasion of England was never imminent. A close blockade of Brest [the nearest big enemy port] was, therefore, considered . . . neither necessary nor desirable." Instead, the French were encouraged to leave their ports at the least favourable time of year, winter. "In winter, therefore, Brest was left open, and British squadrons withdrawn from the arduous task of close-watching the iron-bound Breton coast. The winter months were spent in training and recruiting the ships' companies at the main depot – Portsmouth . . . (3)" In this way, the Admiralty hoped to tempt the French ships out, and destroy them in battle.

Admiral
Collingwood
But with the renewal of war with France in 1803, and threat of invasion, the Admiralty at once went back to close-blockading Brest. Admiral Collingwood had this important job. He wrote in 1803: "I am lying off the entrance of Brest Harbour, to watch the motions of the French fleet. Our information respecting them is very vague, but we know they have four or five and twenty great ships, which makes it necessary to be alert and keep our eyes open at all times. I therefore bid adieu to snug beds and comfortable naps at night, never lying down but in my clothes.

"The Admiral [commanding the Channel squadron] sends all the ships to me, and cruises off Ushant [an island near Brest] by himself. But with a westerly wind it is impossible with one squadron to prevent ships getting into Brest Harbour, for it has two entrances, very distant from each other. One . . . is entirely out of view. I take the utmost pains to prevent all access, and an anxious time I have of it, what with tides and rocks, which have more danger in them than a battle once a week (4)."

Close
Blockades
A House of Commons member agreed that the close blockades of Brest and other French bases were now vital to keep French armies from getting over to England: "The French have got upwards of a thousand [transport] vessels at Boulogne. I am glad to find they are shut up there . . . I wish we had any means of knowing when they intended to come out. I know this much, however, that they cannot all get out in one day, or in one night either . . . Have we not all the enemy's ports blockaded from Toulon to Flushing? Are we not able to cope, anywhere, with any force the enemy dares to send out against us, and do we not even

14

outnumber them at every one of those ports we have blockaded (5)?"

Ignoring all the close blockades of his ports, Napoleon was anxious to start his invasion of England. He urged Admiral Ganteaume at Brest to get his fleet to sea: "With 21 ships, I hope you will be in a position to do something . . . Your sortie has struck the English with great terror. They know well that, having all the seas to defend, a squadron escaping from Brest could do them incalculable harm [by throwing off other blockades]. And, if you could carry . . . 16,000 men and 500 horses to Ireland, the result would be fatal to our enemies. Tell me if you think you can be ready, and what are the probabilities of success."

Impatiently, Napoleon went on: "I do not understand why your ships do not get under way every day to manoeuvre in the roadstead [sea lane]. What possible danger is there in doing that? . . . I do not know the roadstead of Brest well enough to know if a squadron of five ships could manoeuvre there, and at your signal put itself in battle order for the different evolutions. If that is practicable, why isn't it done? I have caused these manoeuvres to be carried out by the Boulogne flotilla, with excellent results . . . (6)"

Napoleon told Admiral Ganteaume to speed up training: "Be frank: how many ships have you which clear for action well? The hammocks are badly stowed. Everything is not prepared as it should be! In short, nothing is unimportant for success. Why do you not make, every week at least, the signal to clear for action, and why do you not then visit the ships and see how badly it can be carried out . . . ?

"I have no more flag-officers. I should like to make some rear-admirals, but I want to choose the most promising, without regard to seniority. Send me a list of a dozen officers worthy of being made rear-admirals, having the qualities necessary to deserve promotion, and above all still in the vigour of life . . . (7)."

While Napoleon and Ganteaume exchanged letters, Collingwood was hard at work trying to close-blockade Brest. Politicians had little idea how hard this was in the rough winter weather: "To sail from one blockaded port and enter another, where the whole fleet is, without being seen, does not come within the comprehension of the city politicians. Their idea is that we are like sentinels standing at a door, who . . . intercept all who attempt to go into it.

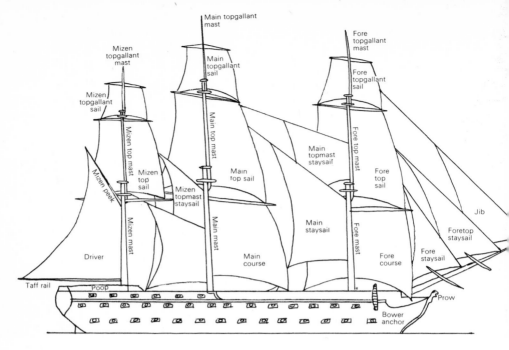

Main topgallant mast

Mizen topgallant mast

Fore topgallant mast

Main topgallant sail

Fore topgallant sail

Mizen topgallant sail

Mizen top mast

Main top mast

Fore top mast

Main topmast staysail

Fore topmast staysail

Mizen top sail

Main top sail

Fore top sail

Mizen topmast staysail

Mizen peak

Jib

Main staysail

Foretop staysail

Mizen mast

Main mast

Fore mast

Driver

Main course

Fore course

Fore staysail

Taff rail

Poop

Prow

Bower anchor

Diagram showing the rigging and masts of a battleship in Nelson's day

But so long as the ships are at sea they are content, little considering that every one of the blasts which we endure lessens the security of the country. The last cruise disabled five large ships, and two more lately; several of them must be docked.

"If the country gentlemen do not make it a point to plant oaks wherever they will grow, the time will not be very distant when, to keep our navy, we must depend entirely on captures from the enemy . . . I wish everybody thought on this subject as I do. They would not walk through their farms without a pocketful of acorns to drop in the hedge-sides . . . (8)"

Admiral Nelson
Further south, Admiral Nelson's Mediterranean squadron was trying to blockade the French fleet in Toulon. This was a hard task, too. Nelson had too few ships; the winter weather was taking its toll. But:

"I never saw a fleet altogether so well officered and manned. Would to God the ships were half as good! . . . My crazy ships are getting into a very indifferent state, and others will soon follow. The finest ones in the service would soon be destroyed by such terrible weather. I know well enough that if I were to go in to

16

View of the French naval base at Rochefort

Malta [a British base], I should save the ships during this bad season. But if I am to watch the French, I must be at sea; and if at sea, must have bad weather. And if the ships are not fit to stand bad weather, they are useless. Unfortunately in bad weather I am always seasick (9)."

But if anyone could manage the task, it was surely the experienced Nelson. An officer beloved both by his men and his officers—if not always by the Admiralty—he was already a famous sailor. He had smashed the French fleet at the famous Battle of the Nile in 1798, and again at Copenhagen in 1801.

Most ordinary sailors grumbled at the monotony of blockade duty, with its weeks at sea with nothing to do but scan the horizon. John Nicol sometimes joined raiding parties to the French coast near Toulon: "I was constantly on shore, when any service was to be done in destroying stores, spiking guns, blowing up batteries, and enjoyed it much. We carried off all the brass guns . . . Those metal ones that were near the edge of the rocks we threw into the sea. This was excellent sport to us. But we were forced to leave it, and sail to Gibraltar for water and provisions . . . (10)"

Blockade duty

17

A naval captain wrote in June, 1804: "Though Lord Nelson is indefatigable in keeping the sea, there are . . . many reasons that make it possible for the French to escape through the Mediterranean . . . First, then, he does not cruise upon his rendezvous. Second, I have consequently repeatedly known him from a week to three weeks, and even a month, unfound by ships sent to reconnoitre . . . Thirdly, he is occasionally obliged to take the whole squadron in to water, a great distance from Toulon. Fourthly, since I came away, the French squadron got out in his absence, and cruised off Toulon several days. And at last, when he came out, he only got sight of them at a great distance, to see them arrive at their own harbour.

"From all this I draw one general conclusion – that it is very possible for them to escape him. Upon the last occasion they might have got to the West Indies, or elsewhere, without the possibility of discovery (11)." This, indeed, was soon to happen.

"They have ten sail of the line at Toulon, one at Cadiz, four, I think, at Ferrol, six at Rochefort, and twenty, you say, at Brest, making in all one-and-forty sail of the line. If they pass Lord Nelson, they can relieve Cadiz (which is only blockaded by two frigates), Ferrol, Rochefort; and if in their way to Brest you meet them some morning, when they are attempting a grand junction, I shall not be surprised . . . (12)"

England in danger

As 1805 opened, England was in real danger. "Never, perhaps," wrote Nelson, "was Europe more critically situated than at this moment, and never was the probability of universal monarchy more nearly being realized than in the person of the Corsican [*i.e.* Napoleon] . . . Prussia is trying to be destroyed last; Spain is little better than a province of France; Russia does nothing on the grand scale.

"Would to God these great powers reflected that the boldest measures are the safest! They allow small states to fall, and to serve the enormous power of France, without appearing to reflect that every kingdom which is annexed to France makes their existence, as independent states, more precarious . . . (13)"

Betsy Fremantle's husband was a naval captain who returned to sea in the emergency of 1805. Betsy wrote, "I begin to be half alarmed at the attempt to invade which is now daily expected to take place . . . These horrid French are such desperate wretches that I quite dread their attack, tho' I trust it will prove unsuccessful (14)."

In Portsmouth, where she was visiting her husband, they were surprised to see "a great concourse of people on the beach, the yeomanry out, guns frequently fired, signals made, the telegraphs at work, and many sails in sight. On enquiring I was told it was supposed the French were affecting a landing, as numbers of the flat-bottom boats were seen making towards the shore." "This created a very great alarm," wrote Betsy, but next day she was happy to hear "that a fleet of coasters who had been becalmed at the back of the Isle of Wight had occasioned our alarm (15)." Everyone relaxed. *French attempt to land*

There was much popular hatred for the French. Priests tiraded against the French from their pulpits: "You will not, I think, be guilty of a breach of Christian charity in the use of even harsh language when you explain to your congregations the cruelties which the French have used in every country they have invaded . . . *Hatred of French*

"They everywhere strip the poorest of everything they possess. They plunder their cottages, and they set them on fire when the plunder is exhausted. They torture the owners to discover their wealth, and they put them to death when they have none to discover. They violate females of all ages . . . Can there be men in Great Britain of so base a temper, so maddened by malignity, so cankered by envy, so besotted by folly, so stupefied as to their own safety, as to abet the designs of such an enemy? (16)"

The cartoonist George Cruickshank wrote that "every town was, in fact, a sort of garrison. In one place you might hear the tattoo of some youths learning to beat the drum; at another some march or national air being practised upon the fife; and every morning at five o'clock the bugle horn was sounded through the streets, to call the Volunteers to a two-hour drill, and the same again in the evening (17)."

Everyone feared an invasion. French battleships lay restlessly at anchor in their blockaded ports. Britain must now put her trust in her ships and men, and hope to draw the enemy out into a great battle at sea. Only in this way could the danger be permanently dealt with.

2 Pressed into Service

WHAT KIND OF NAVY was it, that was soon to fight the French in *British* the greatest naval battle ever known? Britain was very proud of her *Navy* long seafaring traditions; yet somehow the Admiralty could never seem to find enough recruits for the ships. Conditions at sea were notoriously bad. The discipline was harsh; the hygiene poor; the pay low; the diet appalling; the services primitive. The only way men could be found for naval service, especially in wartime, was by the brutal system of "impressment" or forced recruitment.

In theory, only merchant seamen, fishermen and watermen were liable to be pressed. But a ruthless press gang, paid by results, might impress men and boys who had never been to sea before. A victim could sometimes bribe the press gang to let him go. Gentlemen, or those who dressed as such, were usually exempt. During a great national emergency, such as led up to the battle of Trafalgar, the Admiralty might hold a "hot press" in which all grown boys and men were liable to be conscripted.

Here is an impressment order issued to naval captains by the *Impressment* Admiralty in 1803. Each captain must "select from the crew of his *order* Majesty's ship under your command a sufficient number of trusty and well disposed men to man three boats, with as many marines and petty officers as you may judge necessary to send in each, under the orders of a lieutenant, to whom you will deliver a press warrant . . . And you are likewise to select sixteen steady marines that may be trusted to go on shore to stop the avenues leading up to the country . . .

"You will endeavour to have previous communication with one of his Majesty's Justices of the Peace for the district, applying

21

Opposite A press gang at work: "For God's sake, gentlemen, don't drag me like a thief!" Woman: "For goodness' sake, dear your honour, set him free, he maintains his father, mother, sister and wife!" Naval officer: "Let them starve and be damned. The King wants men. Haul him on board, you dogs."

A waterman being pressed into naval service at Tower Hill on the morning of his wedding day

to him to back the warrants, taking especial care to cause as little alarm as possible. On the boats returning to the ships, you will make a return to me of the number and qualities of the men that may have been impressed . . . Given, &c., *Culloden* in Torbay, 25th April, 1803. By command of the Rear-Admiral (18)."

One seaman recalled a narrow escape from the press gang: "I landed at Gosport [near Portsmouth], and proceeded on my road to the boundary of the town, where the soldiers stopped me. But, after showing them my liberty [leave] ticket, and having a little parley with them, I was allowed to go on. I bent my course forward until I reached Fareham . . . Being aware that a press gang was lurking about that neighbourhood, I felt very much inclined to give them a little trouble. I had gone nearly through the town un-observed by them, but at length the alarm was given that a sailor was making good his way in full sail to London . . . Two members of that worthless set of body-snatchers set out in pursuit. I could, by keeping a good lookout, observe their movements and I walked sharply on. They commenced running. I did the same, and kept well on until I arrived at an inn by the roadside, when I thought proper to stop, and let them come up with me.

"I did not take any notice of them, nor show any appearance of alarm. But, supposing I was a prize, one of them grappled me on the starboard, and the other on the larboard side, by the collar of my jacket, demanding the name of the ship I belonged to . . . On coolly showing them my liberty ticket, they showered a broadside of curses on me for giving them such a run, and quietly left me to pursue my journey.

"After this, however, I had to contend with the land sharks, for on my arrival at Alton I was stopped by a party of soldiers, to whose inspection I had again to exhibit my ticket of leave . . . Thus for thirty miles from the sea port was a poor seaman hunted by this detestable set . . . The inducement held out to each of these men-stealers is five pounds for each seaman they may capture (19)."

Another sailor escaped the press gang by posing as a gentleman of means: "When we arrived at Gravesend, a man-of-war's boat came on board to press any Englishmen there might be on board . . . So we stowed ourselves away among some bags of cotton, where we were almost smothered, but could hear every word that was said." Fortunately, the lieutenant left the brig without making much of a search. "When the boat left the vessel we crept from our hiding hole, and not long after a custom-house officer came on board. When we cast anchor, as I had a suit of long clothes in my chest . . . I put them on immediately, and gave the custom-house officer half a guinea for the loan of his cocked hat and powdered wig. The long gilt-headed cane was included in the bargain.

Another escape

"I got a waterman to put me on shore. I am confident my own father, had he been alive, could not have known me with my cane in my hand, cocked hat, and bushy wig. I inquired of the waterman the way to the inn where the coach set out for London . . . All those precautions were necessary. Had the waterman suspected me to be a sailor, he would have informed the press gang in one minute. The waiters at the inn would have done the same (20)."

Naval captains had to report to the Admiralty the results of their press ganging. Here is the report of one in 1803: "Sir, in pursuance of your order, I went last night to Dartmouth with the officers and men previously directed, and made a strict search in all the public houses, and in every other place where there might be a probability of success. I dispatched at the same time a party to examine all the vessels afloat.

"I am sorry to say the result of all these endeavours only produced two men. This is, I imagine, to be accounted for by the same duty having been several times performed at Dartmouth since the first breaking out of the impress, which has made the seamen too wary to be suddenly caught (21)."

Some naval captains were very unscrupulous in their methods. One sailor, who wrote under the pen-name "Jack Nastyface", remembered how "When we were convoying an East Indian fleet from England to the Tropic, one of them happened to have an excellent band on board. Our captain took a fancy into his head that he would have some of them. So, before he took leave of his convoy, he . . . sent a lieutenant and boat's crew to press the two best musicians. This they did, and brought them on board, to increase our band for the captain's amusement—and not to strengthen our force to engage any enemy! (22)"

Recruits were often made to sign a paper on arrival. This rambling one was signed by a recruit to Nelson's ship, the *Victory*: "I Gaetan Loyagalo, do make an oath that I am by trade a bricklayer, and to the best of my information and belief was born in Milan, and am entirely free from all engagements, and that I have no rupture nor was ever troubled with fits, and that I am in no wise disabled by lameness or otherwise but have the perfect use of my limbs, and that I have voluntarily enlisted myself to serve his Britannic Majesty King George III in his Royal Marine Forces during the present war, under an agreement that I shall be discharged at the end of it, and a passage free of expense to the Mediterranean (23)." Loyagalo could not write, so he put his mark at the bottom of the paper.

The new recruit then took the oath of allegiance, promising to serve the King faithfully "in defence of his person, Crown and dignity against all his enemies and oppressors whatsoever." Finally a certificate was issued and signed by Nelson. "These are to certify that Gaetan Loyagalo aforesaid, aged 27 years, 5 feet 10

A woman faints as her husband is dragged off by the press gang (cartoon by Thomas Rowlandson)

inches high, sandy hair, grey eyes, freckled complexion, came before me and declared he had voluntarily enlisted himself to serve his B[ritannic] Majesty King George III in his Royal Marine Forces. He is therefore duly enlisted, and the second and third Articles of War against mutiny and sedition are likewise read to him, and he has taken the oath of fidelity mentioned in the said Articles of War . . . (24)" The new marine now received five guineas' bounty, and was taken to the purser to be issued with the regulation naval dress.

Here is a list of four men impressed about the same time by crews from H.M.S. *Thunderer* (25):

Men's Names	Age	Remarks
Thomas Perring	27	Served his time as a rope-maker; has never been at sea; worked in Woolwich yard five years; came to Brixham to see his parents.

Rob Lane	31	Works as a blacksmith at Brixham; never at sea; says he is troubled with fits and sickness.
John Harris	22	Works as a shipwright; has property belonging to him at Newton Abbot.
James Moffett	24	A fisherman belonging to Brixham; says he has a protection for the *Endeavour* sloop now laying at Dartmouth.

Captains' views

Naval captains did not think much of pressed men. These are some comments gathered from their letters and reports (26):

"Blackguards."

"Sorry poor creatures that don't earn half the victuals they eat."

"Sad thievish creatures."

"Not a rag left but was of such a nature as had to be destroyed."

"150 on board, the greatest part of them sorry fellows."

"Unfit for service and a nuisance to the ship."

"Twenty-six poor souls, but three of them seamen. Ragged and half dead."

"Landsmen, boys, incurables and cripples. Sad wretches great part of them are."

"More fit for an hospital than the sea."

"All the rag-tag that can be picked up."

The press was never held after England's victory over France in 1815. It was legally abolished in 1833.

Jack Nastyface

Not all naval recruits were pressed; many were enthusiastic volunteers. One was "Jack Nastyface", a sailor whose anonymous memoirs contain a remarkably vivid and detailed account of life at sea in Nelson's day. On 9th May, 1805, Jack went to the naval recruiting centre at Tower Hill, London. But once on board ship, "I began to repent of the rash step I had taken. But it was of no avail . . . After having been examined by the doctor and reported seaworthy, I was ordered down the hold, where I remained all night with my companions in wretchedness, and the rats running over us in numbers.

"When released, we were ordered into the admiralty tender which was to convey us to the Nore [base in the Thames estuary].

A brawl near the naval recruiting centre at Tower Hill, London

Here we were called over by name, nearly two hundred. [These included] a number of Lord Mayor's men, a term given to those who are sent on board by any of the City magistrates for a street frolic or night charge ... We were ordered down in the hold and the gratings put over us, as well as a guard of marines placed round the hatchway with their muskets loaded and fixed bayonets ...

"In this place we spent the day and the following night huddled together, for there was not room to sit or stand separate. Indeed we were in a pitiable plight, for numbers of them were sea-sick, some retching, others were smoking, whilst many were so overcome by the stench that they fainted for want of air. As soon as the officer on deck understood that the men below were overcome with foul air, he ordered the hatches to be taken off . . .

"Daylight broke in upon us . . . A wretched appearance we cut, for scarcely any of us were free from filth and vermin. We had by this time arrived at the Nore and were all ordered on deck . . . Boats from the receiving ship were alongside to take us away from the tender and place us on board those ships, where we were supplied with slops, the price of which is stopped from our pay by the purser, and in due time we were transferred and distributed among the different ships . . . (27)"

Good and
bad men "A man-of-war," remarked another sailor, "may justly be styled an epitome of the world, in which there is a sample of every character, some good men as well as bad, but in general the latter are predominant—here are (in disguise) highwaymen, burglars, pickpockets, debauchees, adulterers, gamesters, lampooners, bastard-getters, imposters, panders, parasites, ruffians, hypocrites, threadworn beaux jack-a-dandies. These, with their roses faded and their lilies soiled, walk the deck in utter contempt, dejected and forlorn, with the old tarpaulin jacket, dirty shirt and pad straw hat (28)."

These were some of the men who, within a few months, were to be fighting in the greatest naval battle the world had then known.

3 Nelson's Navy

AFTER SIGNING ON, Jack Nastyface was excited to learn that he was to join Nelson's fleet, probably in the 74-gun *Revenge*. But this turned out no better. The seaman's day was hard: "Our crew was divided into two watches, starboard and larboard. When one was on deck the other was below. For instance, the starboard watch would come on at eight o'clock at night which is eight bells. At half-past is called one bell, and so on. Every half hour is a bell, as the hour glass is turned, and the messenger sent to strike the bell which is generally affixed near the fore-hatchway. It now became the duty of the officer on deck to see that the log line is run out, to ascertain how many knots the ship goes an hour, which is entered in the log book with any other occurrences which may take place during the watch (29)." *A seaman's day*

Another seaman-writer, Samuel Stokes, sailed in a ship that was "noted for her wicked principles." He wrote: "I am now in a ship where I can give full scope to every sinful practice, for if ever there was anything on earth that deserved to be called a hell, this ship was one. But she was just what suited me, for I was only fit companion for the worst in the ship, and drunkenness and swearing was to me a delight . . . *Ship of sin*

"The sins of this ship was equal to the sins of Sodom, especially on the day we was paid, for we had on board thirteen women more than the number of our ship's company, and not fifty of them married women. Our ship's company, I think, was very near 800 men. We sailed from Cowsand Bay two or three days after the ship was paid, and left the bomb boat men to repent that ever they trusted the *Dreadnought* a penny. It was calculated the ship's company

29

Above "Cold blows the wind, and the rain's coming on." A dismal picture of a ship's watch, by the cartoonist George Cruickshank

owed £2,000 and I believe they never got so many farthings (30)."

Many boys entered the navy between the ages of eight and twelve. Samuel Leech thought that a youngster could hardly have a worse upbringing: "There are few worse places than a man-of-war for the favourable development of the moral character in a boy. Profanity in its most revolting aspect; licentiousness in its most shameful and beastly garbs; vice in the worst Proteus-like shapes, abound there . . . (31)"

John Nicol was shocked at conditions aboard his first ship, the *Conditions* 20-gun *Proteus*, which was bound for New York. "I was appointed cooper, which was a great relief to my mind, as I messed with the steward in his room. I was thus away from the crew. I had been much annoyed . . . from the swearing and loose talking of the men in the tender . . . To add to the disagreeable situation I was in, the troops were very unhealthy. We threw overboard every morning a soldier or a sheep . . . We sailed with our convoy direct for Quebec. Upon our arrival, the men, having been so long on salt provisions, made too free with the river water, and were almost all seized with flux. The *Proteus* was upon this account laid up for six weeks, during which time the men were in hospital (32)."

A naval squadron on a long cruise would carry an abundance of *Livestock* livestock, such as bullocks, pigs, sheep, goats, geese, ducks, turkeys, and chickens. "Many of the creatures, being domesticated, were spared the general slaughter and had names given to them by the tars [sailors]. There was Billy the goat, Jenny the cow, Tom the sheep, Jack the goose, and many others. Jenny the cow, after being two years on board, ran dry, and therefore was killed . . . Poor Tom the sheep was killed by lighting, and I know not what became of Billy.

"As for Jack the goose, he saw them all out, and I believe, was in the ship when I left her. It was a very tame creature, so remarkably so, that he would come out of his coop, and join the assemblage of forcastlemen, when they have been in a group, talking about anything and seemed quite at home amongst them (33)."

Meals were generally dull and monotonous. The diet was poor. *Food* Breakfast was served at about eight bells: "This meal usually consists of burgoo made of coarse oatmeal and water; others will have scotch coffee which is burnt bread boiled in some water and sweetened with sugar. This is generally cooked in a hook-pot in the

Opposite Sailors and their women enjoying themselves below decks while the ship lies at anchor

Left to right A midshipman with a ship's log and sextant; an ordinary seaman ashore; a seaman aboard ship; a purser; a captain

galley where there is a range. Nearly all the crew have one of these pots, a spoon and a knife; for these are things indispensable.

"There are also basins, plates, *etc.*, which are kept in each mess. [The mess] consists of eight persons who berth in between two of the guns on the lower deck, where there is a board placed which swings with the rolling of the ship and answers for a table. It sometimes happens that a lurch will dash all the crockery to pieces; they are then obliged to eat out of wooden or tin utensils, until they come into harbour, where they can get another supply (34)."

The meat, preserved in salt, was virtually uneatable: "It needed rather a magician than a cook to make it eatable. It was of a stony hardness, fibrous, shrunken, dark, gristly, and glistening with salt crystals . . . The salt pork was generally rather better than the beef, but the sailors could carve fancy articles, such as boxes, out of either meat. The flesh is said to have taken a good polish, like some close-grained wood (35)." This was the weekly diet for each man laid down by the Navy Victualling Board:

32

	Biscuit	Beer	Beef	Pork	Pease	Oatmeal	Butter	Cheese
Sunday	1 lb	1 gall	—	1 lb	$\frac{1}{2}$ pt	—	2 oz	—
Monday	1 lb	1 gall	—	—	—	1 pt	2 oz	4 oz
Tuesday	1 lb	1 gall	2 lb	—	—	—	—	—
Wednesday	1 lb	1 gall	—	—	$\frac{1}{2}$ pt	1 pt	2 oz	4 oz
Thursday	1 lb	1 gall	—	1 lb	$\frac{1}{2}$ pt	—	—	—
Friday	1 lb	1 gall	—	—	$\frac{1}{2}$ pt	1 pt	2 oz	4 oz
Saturday	1 lb	1 gall	2 lb	—	—	—	—	—

The biscuits were invariably full of weevils: "The most common custom was to leave the creatures to their quiet and to eat the biscuits at night, when the eye saw not and the tender heart was spared (36)."

Sometimes the crew took revenge on their cooks: "On some occasions he is subject to censure or punishment by his mess mates, for not attending to the dinner properly, or suffering the utensils of his department to be in a dirty condition. Justice in these cases is awarded by picking a jury of cooks from different messes, for it falls to the lot of each man in a mess to act as cook in his turn (37)."

The sailors had few chances for a feast. Jack Nastyface remembered one "fine opportunity for our seamen to feast themselves on bullock's liver, or Torbay goose as they call it, for this, fried with salt pork, makes not only a relishing, but a delicious meal for a mess. Indeed, it has frequently occurred that our captain would, when we were killing a bullock at sea, send orders to the butcher for his cook to be supplied with a plate of the liver, to be fried for his table. At Torquay, a town in Torbay, it has been usual in wartime to kill a supply of beef for the Channel fleet, and then we often partook of this very excellent dish, as the livers were plentiful (38)."

The British sailor was famous for his love of "grog" (watered rum), of which he had a free tot every day. "After punishment, the boatswain's mate pipes to dinner, it being eight bells or twelve o'clock . . . This is the pleasantest part of the day, as at one bell the fifer is called to play *Nancy Dawson* or some other lively tune, a well known signal that the grog is ready to be served out. Every man and boy is allowed a pint, that is one gill of rum and three of water, to which is added lemon acid sweetened with sugar (39)."

The cook took for himself an extra portion of grog. "This is called the over-plus, and generally comes to the double of a man's allowance. Thus the cook can take upon himself to be the man of consequence, for he has the opportunity of inviting a friend to partake of a glass, or of paying any little debt he may have contracted . . . It is grog which pays debts, and not money, in a man-of-war (40)." "Grog" was named after Admiral Vernon, who was nicknamed "Old Grogham" on account of his waterproof boat-cloak of that type:

> *A mighty bowl on deck he drew*
> *And filled it to the brink;*
> *Such drank the Burford's gallant crew*
> *And such the Gods shall drink;*
> *The sacred robe which Vernon wore*
> *Was drenched with the same;*
> *And hence its virtues guard our shore*
> *And Grog derives its name.*

Cooking a meal in the ship's galley

Samuel Leech remarked that, "To be drunk is considered by almost every sailor as the acme of sensual bliss . . . Some of our men who belonged to boats' crews provided themselves with bladders. If left ashore by their officers a few moments they would slip into the first grocery, fill their bladders, and return with the spoil. Once by the ship's side, the favourable moment was seized to pass the interdicted bladders into the portholes, to some watchful shipmate, by whom it was carefully secreted to be drunk at the first opportunity . . .

"At Christmas the ship presented a scene such as I had never imagined. The men were permitted to have their 'full swing'. Drunkenness ruled the ship. Nearly every man, with most of the officers, was in a state of beastly intoxication at night. Here, some were fighting but were so insensibly drunk they hardly knew whether

Sailors enjoying themselves in their quarters below decks

they struck the guns or their opponents ... All were laughing, cursing, swearing or hallooing; confusion reigned in glorious triumph. It was the very chaos of humanity (41)."

John Nicol told how some men had mutinied when their rum ration had been cut: "While we lay in Leith Roads, a mutiny broke out in the *Defiance* ... The cause was, their captain gave them five-water grog; now the common thing is three-waters. The weather was cold; the spirit thus reduced was, as the mutineers called it, 'as thin as muslin,' and quite unfit to keep out the cold. No seaman could endure this in cold climates. Had they been in hot latitudes, they would have been happy to get it thus, for the sake of the water (42)."

Smuggling Jack Nastyface complained that seamen who tried to smuggle 36 goods home were ruthlessly punished. Yet many officers did just

Ship's officers enjoying a glass of port at the captain's table (Thomas Rowlandson)

that: "On board the different ships, there were numerous packages, which had been shipped at Flushing, and no doubt but they were intended to be smuggled into England . . . The bread room of our ship was crowded with them, directed for different officers holding high rank, both in army and navy, and may have been intended as presents or for their own use, but they did not pay the duty. These packages consisted of sets of Hamburg china, and table services, down for beds, spirits, and various other articles of foreign produce . . . Contrast this with a seaman's bringing home the most trifling article, as a present to a relation or friend: the poor fellow is pounced upon immediately (43)."

Jack Nastyface often wrote of the bad treatment which the officers meted out to their men. The most junior rank of officer was midshipman; these were especially unpopular. Jack knew one

Officers' cruelty

"Tars carousing"–by George Cruickshank

whose "sole delight was to insult the feelings of the seamen, and furnish pretexts to get them punished . . . He was a youth not more than twelve or thirteen years of age. I have often seen him get on the carriage of a gun, call a man to him, and kick him about the thighs and body . . . and these, although prime seamen, at the same time dared not murmur.

"It was ordained, however, by Providence, that his reign of terror and severity should not last; for during the engagement, he was killed on the quarter-deck by a grapeshot, his body greatly mutilated, his entrails being driven and scattered against the larboard side. Nor were there any lamentations for his fate . . . His death was hailed as the triumph over an enemy! (44)"

Jack Nastyface remarked that "any person who has been on board a ship of war must be aware that discipline and subordination is necessary. But the extent to which cruelty was carried on under the name of discipline, on board many ships during the late war, is not generally known. Nor will a British public believe that any body of men would submit to such marks of degradation as they were compelled to undergo. It was partially known at Somerset

Nelson (upper right) and his sailors feasting after their great victory over the French at the Nile

House by the different ships' logs.

"But the real crime, if any, was not, it is believed, therein set down; for there it came under the head of 'disobedience' or under a peculiar article of war which run as follows: 'All crimes not capital shall be punished according to the customs and manners used at sea.' This article shelters the captains in the navy in resorting to almost any mode of punishment they may think proper (45)."

Each day at sea, the officers handed out rough discipline: *Punishment* "About eleven o'clock or six bells, when any of the men are in irons, or on the black list, the boatswains' mates are ordered to call all hands. The culprits are then brought forward by the master-at-arms . . . All hands being now mustered, the captain orders the man to strip: he is then seized [*i.e.* lashed] to a grating by the wrists and knees. His crime is then mentioned and the prisoner may plead. But in nineteen cases out of twenty he is flogged for the most trifling offence or neglect, such as not hearing the watch called at night (46)."

The most serious punishment in the Navy at that time, apart from death, was flogging through the fleet. Jack Nastyface gave a terrible

A young naval officer and seaman accused of smuggling by a customs officer

Flogging through the fleet account of one time at Spithead. Four impressed seamen had tried to desert: "They were tried by a court-martial and sentenced to receive three hundred lashes each through the fleet . . . The man is placed in a launch under the care of the master-at-arms and a doctor. Then a capstan bar is rigged fore and aft, to which the poor fellow is lashed by his wrists and, for fear of hurting him – humane creatures! – there is a stocking put over each, to prevent him from tearing the flesh off in his agonies.

"When all is ready, the prisoner is stripped and seized to the

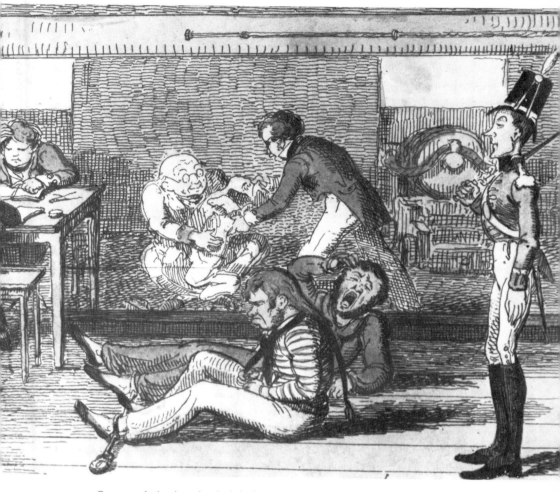

Seamen chained to the deck in irons for getting drunk

capstan bar. Punishment commences by the officer, after reading
the sentence of the court martial, ordering the boatswains' mates
to do their duty. The cat-of-nine tails is applied to the bare back . . .
At about every six lashes a fresh boatswain's mate is ordered to
relieve the executioner of his duty, until the prisoner has received
perhaps twenty-five lashes. He is then cast loose, and allowed to
sit down with a blanket rolled round him and is conveyed to the
next ship, escorted by the vast number of armed boats, accom-
panied by the dreadful music, the *Rogues' March*.

41

The entire ship's company is drawn up to watch a sailor being flogged
(cartoon by George Cruickshank)

"In this manner he is conveyed from ship to ship, receiving alongside of each a similar number of stripes with the cat, until the sentence is completed . . . Every kind of method is made use of to enable him to bear it, such as by pouring wine down his throat. The doctor will then feel his pulse, and often pronounces that the man is unable to bear more. He is then taken, most usually insensible, to what is termed the *sick bay*, and, if he recovers, he is told he will have to receive the remainder of his punishment. When there are many ships in the fleet at the time of the court martial, this ceremony, if the prisoner can sustain it, will last nearly half the day (47)."

Starting   "Starting" was a common form of punishment: "This may be carried to a great extent of torture, as every boatswain's mate carries a rope's-end in his pocket . . . The man is ordered to pull off his jacket and sometimes his waistcoat if he has one on at the time. The boatswain's mate then commences beating him and continues

Punishing a seaman with a rope's end

to do so until he is ordered to stop, or unless his arm is tired, and then another boatswain's mate is called to go on with the ceremony . . . This punishment is so common that no mention is made of it even in the log book . . . Few men in wartime can escape the above mode of punishment (48)."

"Gagging" was the penalty for talking back to an officer. "The man is placed in a sitting position, with both legs put in irons, and his hands secured behind him. His mouth is then forced open, and an iron bolt put across, well secured behind his head. A sentinel is placed over him with his drawn bayonet, and in this situation he remains until the Captain thinks proper to release him . . . (49)" *Gagging*

Disaffection among British sailors showed itself dramatically in two mutinies in 1797. The first took place at the naval base of Spithead, in April, where the Channel fleet of Lord Bridport refused to put to sea, at least unless an enemy appeared. The second took place at the Nore in April, 1797, led by a sailor called Richard *Nore and Spithead mutinies*

The mutiny at the Nore: Richard Parker hands a list of grievances to an Admiral

Parker. But the mutineers did not carry out their threat to blockade the River Thames, and fell instead to quarrelling among themselves. The mutiny was savagely put down, and Parker was hanged the following July.

Pay day   The sailors indeed had much to grumble about. They were paid very irregularly, and often at long intervals. Pay day, when it came, was a great event: "To picture the scene which at this time occurred, is a task almost impossible. In the early part of the day, the Commissioners came on board bringing the money which is paid the ship's crew, with the exception of six months' pay, which it is the rule of the government to hold back from each man.

"The mode of paying is . . . by rotation, on the books. Every man when called, is asked for his hat, which is returned to him with his wages in it and the amount chalked on the rim. There is not perhaps one in twenty who actually knows what he is going to receive, nor does the particular amount seem to be of a matter of much concern . . .

"When paid, they hurry down to their respective berths, redeem their honour with their several ladies and bomb-boat men, and then they turn their thoughts to the Jew pedlars who are ranged round the decks and in the hatchway gratings. They are furnished with every article which will rig out a sailor, never omitting in their parkains a fine large watch and appendages, all warranted, and with which many an honest tar has been taken in (50)."

A sailor had other consolations. On arrival in port, the ships were invaded by boatloads of local women. Often the seamen had not set eyes on a woman for months: "After having moored our ship, swarms of boats came round us . . . A great many of them were freighted with cargoes of ladies, a sight that was truly gratifying, and a grand treat; for our crew, consisting of 600 and upwards, nearly all young men, had seen but one woman on board for eighteen months and that was the daughter of one of the Spanish chiefs, who made no stay on board, but went on shore again immediately.

Welcome cargoes

"So soon as the boats were allowed to come alongside, the seamen flocked down pretty quick, one after the other, and brought

Sailors playing a practical joke on a pedlar of trinkets; few sailors had any money left after the pedlars had visited them on pay day

their choice up, so that in the course of the afternoon, we had about 450 on board (51)."

At Plymouth hospital, visitors were amazed at how many sailor "husbands" some of the nurses claimed to have: "Some of them had several husbands, or men they called by that name, all living on board different ships . . . As there was seldom more than one of these in port at a time, they equally enjoyed the caresses of the pliable spouses in happy ignorance of their dishonour . . . These ladies are exceedingly bold . . . I had a great deal to do to repulse the temptations I met with from these sirens, the more so as I was naturally fond of the society of women (52)."

Advantages of being a seaman
Life in Nelson's navy was generally hard. Yet despite his many complaints about the brutal discipline, poor food, bad pay, its dangers—even Jack Nastyface had some good things to say about it: "To the youth possessing anything of a roving disposition it is attractive. Nay, it is seducing . . . When steadily pursued and with success, it enobles the mind, and the seaman feels himself a man . . . No profession can vie with it, and a British seaman has a right to be proud, for he is incomparable when placed alongside those of any other nation.

"Great Britain can truly boast of her hearts of oak, the floating sinews of her existence, and the high station she holds in the political world. And if she could but once rub out those stains of wanton and torturing punishments, so often unnecessarily resorted to, and abandon the unnatural and uncivilised custom of impressment, then, and not till then, can her navy be said to have got to the truck of perfection (53)."

4 The Nelson Touch

EARLY IN 1805, England was in a perilous situation. Napoleon had gathered an army of invasion, ready to cross the Channel as soon as he could win even temporary control of the sea. His battleships lay at anchor in ports around the Spanish and French coasts, under a precarious blockade. It was imperative that England should win a decisive naval victory before Napoleon collected all his forces together. But how was this to be done?

Off Toulon, Nelson was conducting an "open" blockade. His frigates watched Villeneuve's fleet, while his battleships lay many miles away out of sight. By this means, Nelson hoped to lure Villeneuve out into the open seas where he could do battle with him. Indeed, Napoleon was urging Villeneuve to break out, to try and free other French and Spanish squadrons from their blockades. Villeneuve first tried to put to sea from Toulon in January, but he was driven back by storms. He complained: "I declare to you that ships of the line thus equipped, short-handed, encumbered with troops, with superannuated or bad materials, vessels which lose their masts or sails at every puff of wind, and which in fine weather are constantly engaged in repairing the damages caused by the wind, or the inexperience of their sailors, are not fit to undertake anything (54)."

Thinking that Villeneuve had escaped into the Mediterranean, Nelson combed the seas for hundreds of miles around, only to find out later that bad weather had forced him back into Toulon. The open blockade was resumed. By the end of March, 1805, Villeneuve was ready to try again. Watched by two of Nelson's frigates, he brought his fleet out of Toulon, and was able to give

"Open"
blockade

47

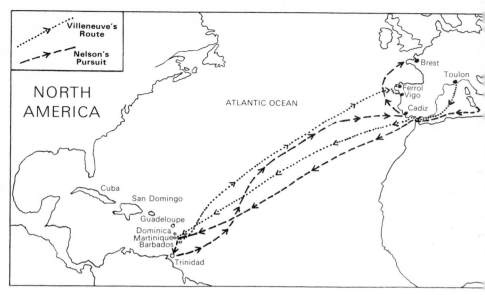

Map showing Nelson's pursuit of Villeneuve across the Atlantic and back, before the Battle of Trafalgar

Nelson the slip. (Nelson had been holding his fleet off Sardinia, to give Villeneuve every chance to come out of Toulon.)

Villeneuve eludes Nelson

But Villeneuve did not make for Egypt, as Nelson had thought. On 9th April, the British garrison at Gibraltar was surprised to see the French fleet sail through the Straits and out into the Atlantic. Villeneuve was making his way round the stormy coast of Portugal to Cadiz. There he chased away the four English blockading battleships, to enable Admiral Gravina to come out with his Spanish ships and join forces with him, following a few days behind.

Quickly gathering all the news he could, the anxious Nelson hurried after Villeneuve, several days behind. He guessed, rightly, that Villeneuve was by now heading out toward the West Indies on the far side of the Atlantic. Villeneuve arrived at Martinique on 16th May, and left on 5th June. Nelson arrived in the West Indies on the 4th June, to find that his quarry had given him the slip. His private diary for the months of June and July shows Nelson full of anxiety that he might not catch Villeneuve in the open sea:

"*21st June, 1805.* Midnight, nearly calm, saw three planks, which I think came from the French fleet. Very miserable, which is

Left Nelson shortly before the Battle of Trafalgar, and *right* as a young naval captain in 1781

very foolish.

"*Wednesday, 17th July, 1805.* Our whole run from Barbuda, day by day, was 3,459 miles: our run from Cape St. Vincent to Barbadoes was 3,227 miles, so that our run back was only 232 miles more than our run out—allowance being made for the difference of the latitudes and longitudes of Barbadoes and Barbuda; average, per day, thirty-four leagues, wanting nine miles.

"*18th July, 1805.* Cape Spartel in sight, but no French fleet, nor any information about them. How sorrowful this makes me, but I cannot help myself (55)."

By 19th July, Nelson was back at Gibraltar, disheartened by his failure to catch up with Villeneuve. At Gibraltar he learned that Villeneuve was sheltering his fleet in Vigo, further up the coast. At least the enemy's whereabouts was now known. Nelson would soon be able to come to grips with him. But first, he had to return to England for a rest after his long months at sea, and make a report to Lord Barham, the shrewd octogenarian First Lord of the Admiralty.

Return to Gibraltar

While chasing the French to the West Indies and back, Nelson

49

had worked out a battle plan for when he caught up with them. It was vital to get a decisive outcome: "The business of an English Commander-in-Chief [is] first to bring an enemy's fleet to battle, on the most advantageous terms to himself (I mean that of laying his ships close on board the enemy, as expeditiously as possible;) and secondly, to continue them there, without separating, till the business is decided . . .

"The Admirals and Captains of the fleet I have the honour to command, will, knowing my precise object, that of a close and decisive battle, supply any deficiency in my not making signals. Therefore, it will only be requisite for me to state, in as few words as possible, the various modes in which it may be necessary for me to obtain my object, on which depends, not only the honour and glory of our Country, but possibly its safety, and with it that of all Europe, from French tyranny and oppression (56)."

Nelson did not believe in spending too much time manoeuvring for position once the enemy's fleet was within range: "If the two fleets are both willing to fight, but little manoeuvring is necessary. The less the better; a day is soon lost in that business. Therefore I will only suppose that the enemy's fleet being to leeward, standing close upon the wind on the starboard tack, and that I am nearly ahead of them, standing on the larboard tack, of course I should weather them. The weather must be supposed to be moderate; for if it be a gale of wind, the manoeuvring of both fleets is but of little avail, and probably no decisive action would take place (57)".

He saw two ways of coming to grips with the enemy fleet. One was to remain "just out of gun-shot, until the van-ship of my line would be about the centre ship of the enemy, then make the signal to wear together, then bear up, engage with all our force the six or five van-ships of the enemy, passing, certainly, if opportunity offered, through their line. This would prevent their bearing up, and the action, from the known bravery and conduct of the Admirals and Captains, would certainly be decisive. The second or third rear-ships of the enemy would act as they please, and our ships would give a good account of them, should they persist in mixing with our ships (58)."

The second method was to "sail directly for their headmost ship, so as to prevent the enemy from knowing whether I should pass to

Sailors taking in a reef

leeward or windward of him. In that situation, I would make the signal to engage the enemy to leeward, and to cut through their fleet about the sixth ship from the van, passing very close; they being on a wind, and you going large, could cut their line when you please. The van-ships of the enemy would, by the time our rear came abreast of the van-ship, be severely cut up, and our van could not expect to escape damage. I would then have our rear ship, and every ship in succession, wear, continue the action with either the van-ship, or second ship, as it might appear most eligible from her crippled state . . .

"This mode pursued, I see nothing to prevent the capture of the five or six ships of the enemy's van. The two or three ships of the enemy's rear must either bear up, or wear . . . In either case, although they would be in a better plight probably than our two van-ships (now the rear), yet they would be separated, and at a distance to leeward, so as to give our ships time to refit . . . By that time, I believe, the battle would . . . be over with the rest of them. Signals from these moments are useless, when every man is disposed to do his duty. The great object is for us to support each other, and

51

Merton Place in Surrey, the home of Lord Nelson

to keep close to the enemy, and to leeward of him.

"If the enemy are running away, then the only signals necessary will be to engage the enemy as arriving up with them; and the other ships to pass on for the second, third, &c., giving, if possible, a close fire into the enemy in passing, taking care to give our ships engaged, notice of your intention (59)."

Nelson arrives home

Nelson arrived home at Merton on 20th August, 1805. There he remained until 13th September. At Merton he had many personal matters to deal with after his long absence. William Beckford, for example, had invited him to stay at his home at Fonthill, but Nelson had to reply: "My dear Mr. Beckford, Many thanks for your kind letter. Nothing could give me more pleasure than paying my respects at Fonthill, but I cannot move at present, as all my family are with me, and my stay is very uncertain; and, besides, I have refused for the present all invitations. Every ship, even the *Victory*, is ordered out, for there is an entire ignorance whether the Ferrol fleet is coming to the northward, gone to the Mediterranean, or cruising for our valuable homeward-bound fleet. I hope they will be met with and annihilated (60)."

Emma Hamilton

52

Lady Emma Hamilton was brokenhearted that her beloved Horatio should be sailing away again so soon. She wrote to Lady

Bolton, a niece of Nelson, "My dear Friend, I am again broken-hearted, as our dear Nelson is immediately going. It seems as though I have had a fortnight's dream, and am awoke to all the misery of this cruel separation. But what can I do? His powerful arm is of so much consequence to his country. But I do, nor cannot say more. My heart is broken (61)."

On 6th September Nelson wrote to Alexander Davison, from Merton: "I hope my absence will not be long, and that I shall soon meet the combined fleets, with a force sufficient to do the job well, for half a victory would but half content me. But I do not believe the Admiralty can give me a force within fifteen or sixteen sail of the line of the enemy; and therefore, if every ship took her opponent, we should have to contend with a fresh fleet of fifteen or sixteen sail of the line. But I will do my best; and I hope God Almighty will go with me. I have much to lose, but little gain; and I go because it's right, and I will serve the Country faithfully (62)."

And on a more personal note: "I send you a Memorandum, which I am sure you will comply with. Poor blind Mrs. Nelson I must assist. This morning a Mr. Brand, an apothecary, called upon me for £113 2s. 6d. as due from my brother Maurice to him. I shall refer him to you, and if it is a just demand, he must have it. I shall leave the bill in St. James's Square – Ever, my dear Davison, your most obliged and affectionate Friend (63)."

Nelson wrote a quick note to his old friend Vice-Admiral Collingwood, "My dear Coll., I shall be with you in a very few days, and I hope you will remain Second in Command. You will change the *Dreadnought* for *Royal Sovereign*, which I hope you will like (64)."

Four days later, on Friday the 13th September, he left Merton. It was to be for the last time. He wrote in his private diary: "At half-past ten drove from dear dear Merton, where I left all which I hold dear in this world, to go to serve my King and country. May the Great God whom I adore enable me to fulfil the expectations of my Country; and if it is His good pleasure that I should return, my thanks will never cease being offered up to the throne of His mercy. If it is His good providence to cut short my days upon earth, I bow with the greatest submission, relying that He will protect those so dear to me, that I may leave behind (65)."

Farewell to Merton

53

The following day, Saturday, Nelson came to the coast: "At six o'clock arrived at Portsmouth, and having arranged all my business, embarked at the Bathing Machines with Mr. Rose and Mr. Canning at two, who dined with me; got on board the *Victory* at St. Helens preparing for sea (66)."

They entry in the *Victory*'s log ran: "At 11.30 a.m., hoisted the Flag of the Right Honourable Lord Viscount Nelson, K.B., Sunday, 15th: 8 a.m. weighed and made sail to the S.S.E. *Euryalus* in company (67)."

Nelson reported his embarkation to William Marsden, Secretary at the Admiralty: "Sir, You will please to acquaint the Lords Commissioners of the Admiralty that I arrived at Portsmouth this morning at six o'clock, and hoisted my Flag on board the *Victory* at this anchorage about noon. The *Royal Sovereign, Defiance*, and *Agamemnon*, are not yet ready for sea, so that I must leave them to follow, the moment they are complete (68)."

On Tuesday 17th, after three days at sea, Nelson wrote again to Lady Hamilton: "Nine o'clock in the morning. Blowing fresh at W.S.W., dead foul wind. I sent, my own dearest Emma, a letter for you, last night, in a Torbay Boat, and gave the man a guinea to put it in the Post Office. We have had a nasty blowing night, and it looks very dirty. I am now signalling the ships at Plymouth to join me; but I rather doubt their ability to get to sea. However, I have got clear of Portland, and have Cawsand Bay and Torbay under the lee. I entreat, my dear Emma, that you will cheer up; and we will look forward to many, many happy years, and be surrounded by our children's children. God Almighty can, when he pleases, remove the impediment [Nelson's existing marriage]. My heart and soul is with you and Horatia [Nelson's daughter by Lady Hamilton]. I got this line ready in case a boat should get alongside (69)."

The next few days at sea were crowded with activity. Nelson was anxious to catch the enemy's combined fleet in the open sea. All his officers and crews were ready and knew exactly what to do. He wrote to James Gambier, British Consul in Lisbon, "Sir, I entreat that it may not be known that I am off Lisbon, for I hope to see our enemy at sea . . . I have further to request that every man which can be raised at Lisbon may be placed for the fleet under my command (70)."

Crowds cheering Nelson at Portsmouth as he is rowed out to the *Victory*
(14th September, 1805)

And to Captain Sutton, H.M. Ship *Amphion*, in the River Tagus, "My dear Sutton, Get every man, in every way, for the Fleet under my command; and beg Mr. Gambier to secure all he can for the Fleet . . . Pray, do not mention my near approach to Cadiz (71)."

Nelson then drew up a general order, telling his scattered ships where to rendezvous in readiness for battle: "To all Junior Flag Officers, and the Captains or Commanders of any of His Majesty's Ships or Vessels, in search of me . . . The Rendezvous of the fleet

The Nelson Touch: Nelson explains his plan of battle to the assembled captains of his fleet

under my command will be between Cape St. Mary's and Cadiz. Ships, therefore, in search of me, not falling in with the fleet off the former place, must approach the latter with the utmost caution; and should I have left Cadiz in pursuit of the enemy, a vessel of war will be stationed off Cape Spartel with information where I am gone to. N.B. Tangier Bay will always give information (72)."

Anxious waiting On the last day of September Nelson wrote to Alexander Davison in England, "Day by day, my dear friend, I am expecting the enemy's fleet to put to sea–every day, hour, and moment; and you may rely that, if it is within the power of man to get at them, that it shall be done . . . Let the battle be when it may, it will never have been surpassed. My shattered frame, if I survive that day, will require rest, and that is all I shall ask for. If I fall on such a glorious occasion, it shall be my pride to take care that my friends shall not blush for me . . . Do not think I am low-spirited on this account, or fancy anything is to happen to me; quite the contrary–my mind is calm, and I have only to think of destroying our inveterate foe . . . Nothing can be finer than the Fleet under my command (73)."

To Lady Hamilton he wrote: "My dearest Emma, It is a relief to me, to take up the pen, and write you a line; for I have had, about four o'clock this morning, one of my dreadful spasms, which has almost enervated me . . . I believe my arrival was most welcome, not only to the Commander of the fleet, but also to every individual in it; and, when I came to explain to them the 'Nelson touch,' it was like an electric shock. Some shed tears, all approved – 'It was new – it was singular – it was simple!'; and, from Admirals downwards, it was repeated – 'It must succeed, if ever they will allow us to get at them. You are, my Lord, surrounded by friends whom you inspire with confidence.' Some may be Judas's; but the majority are certainly much pleased with my commanding them (74)."

Nelson arranged for any news of the enemy's movements out of Cadiz to be signalled to him by a chain of ships: "To Captain Duff, H.M. Ship *Mars*: "As the enemy's fleets may be hourly expected to put to sea from Cadiz, I have to desire that you will keep, with the *Mars*, *Defence* and *Colossus*, from three to four leagues between the fleet and Cadiz, in order that I may get the information from the frigates stationed off that port, as expeditiously as possible. Distant signals to be used, when flags, from the state of the weather, may not readily be distinguished in their colours. If the enemy be out, or coming out, fire guns by day or night, in order to draw my attention. In thick weather, the ships are to close within signal of the *Victory*; one of the ships to be placed to windward, or rather to the eastward of the other two, to extend the distance of seeing; and I have desired Captain Blackwood to throw a frigate to the westward of Cadiz, for the purpose of any easy and early communication (75)." *News of enemy movements*

But Nelson felt desperately short of frigates – "the eyes of the fleet" – to keep a proper lookout for him. He wrote to William Marsden at the Admiralty, "I am sorry ever to trouble their Lordships with anything like a complaint of a want of frigates and sloops. But if the different services require them, and I have them not, those services must be neglected to be performed . . . Never less than eight frigates, and three good fast-sailing brigs, should always be with the fleet to watch Cadiz; and to carry transports in and out to refit it, would take at least ten and four brigs, to do that service well. At present I have only been able to collect two, which makes me very uneasy (76)." *"The eyes of the fleet"*

Captain Blackwood of the *Euryalus* was in command of the frigates watching out for the French fleet. Nelson wrote to him,

"My dear Blackwood, Keep your five frigates, *Weazle*, and *Pickle*, and let me know every movement. I rely on you, that we can't miss getting hold of them, and I will give them such a shaking as they never yet experienced; at least I will lay down my life in the attempt. We are a very powerful Fleet, and not to be held cheap . . . Direct ships bringing information of their coming out, to fire guns every three minutes by the watch, and in the night to fire off rockets, if they have them, from the mast-head. I have nothing more to say, than I hope they will sail tonight (77)."

Plan of attack Nelson wrote out his plan of attack in a memorandum aboard the *Victory* on 9th October: "Thinking it almost impossible to bring a fleet of forty sail of the line into a line of battle in variable winds, thick weather, and other circumstances which must occur, without such a loss of time that the opportunity would probably be lost of bringing the Enemy to Battle in such a manner as to make the business decisive:

"I have therefore made up my mind to keep the fleet in that position of sailing . . . that the order of sailing is to be the order of battle, placing the fleet in two lines of sixteen ships each with an advanced squadron of eight of the fast sailing two decked ships which will always make if wanted a line of twenty four sail, on which ever line the Commander-in-Chief may direct.

"The Second-in-Command will, after my intentions are made known to him have the entire direction of this line to make the attack upon the enemy and to follow up the blow until they are captured or destroy'd . . .

"The whole impression of the British fleet must be, to overpower from two or three ships ahead of their Commander-in-Chief, supposed to be in the centre, to the rear of their fleet. I will suppose twenty sail of the enemy's line to be untouched, it must be some time before they could perform a manoeuvre to bring their force compact to attack any part of the British fleet engaged, or to succour their own ships which indeed would be impossible, without mixing with the ships engaged. Something must be left to chance, nothing is sure in a sea fight beyond all others, shot will carry away the masts and yards of friends as well as foes, but I look with confidence to a victory before the van of the enemy could succour their rear and then that the British fleet would most of them be ready to receive their twenty sail of the line or to pursue them should they endeavour to make off . . .

"The second in command will in all possible things direct the movements of his line by keeping them as compact as the nature of the circumstances will admit and captains are to look to their particular line as their rallying point. But in case signals can neither be seen or perfectly understood no captain can do very wrong if he places his ship alongside that of an enemy . . .

"The Division of the British fleet will be brought nearly within gun shot of the enemy's centre. The signal will most probably then be made for the lee line to bear together to set all their sails, even steering sails, in order to get as quickly as possible to the enemy's line and to cut through beginning from the twelfth ship from the enemy's rear. Some ships may not get through their exact place, but they will always be at hand to assist their friends and if any are thrown round the rear of the enemy they will effectually complete the business of twelve sail of the enemy . . .

"The remainder of the enemy's fleet of 34 sail are to be left to the management of the commander in chief who will endeavour to take care that the movements of the second in command are as little interrupted as is possible (78)."

Nelson was acutely anxious that everyone should understand his plan of attack. For he wanted not just a "splendid victory" but total annihilation of the enemy. He wrote to Admiral Collingwood, ". . . I send you my plan of attack, as far as a man dare venture to guess at the very uncertain position the enemy may be found in. But, my dear friend, it is to place you perfectly at ease respecting my intentions, and to give full scope to your judgment for carrying them into effect. We can, my dear Coll., have no little jealousies. We have only one great object in view, that of annihilating our enemies, and getting a glorious peace for our country. No man has more confidence in another than I have in you (79)." *Nelson's object*

On 18th October, Nelson heard that Villeneuve was at last coming out of Cadiz. A lieutenant aboard the *Victory* wrote: "Our fleet, consisting of 27 sail of the line, four frigates, one schooner, and one cutter (Cadiz bearing east, 16 leagues) received intelligence at 10 a.m. of the enemy's fleet coming out of port. We immediately made all sail, with a very light air at west, towards *"Victory" makes sail*

Cape Trafalgar, to cut off the enemy from entering the Straits of Gibraltar. Light airs prevailed during the whole of the 19th, and until the morning of the 20th, when a fresh breeze sprang up from the southward.

"At daylight not any of the enemy's ships were to be seen from the fleet. But, observing our lookout ships [the Admiral] inquired how the van of the enemy bore, and was answered that ten sail of the line were out of port, and bore north, and the remainder were at anchor. Trafalgar at this time bore E.N.E. 4 leagues.

"The wind increased as the day advanced, and towards noon became squally, with rain at intervals. The fleet hauled off under easy sail to the N.W. In the afternoon the signals were made for 19, 25, and at length 34 sail of the enemy out of port. There could now be no doubt of their intentions to meet us. Their delay had been wholly caused by the light unsteady winds of the 19th, and the squally, unsettled weather of the 20th in the morning.

"His Lordship still kept the fleet from the enemy's sight until they should be a sufficient distance from the land; judging that, if they saw our force (though so much inferior) they might be induced to avoid us. It is probable that they might presume on our numbers, knowing that we had sent six sail of the line into the Mediterranean to water, nor could they know that the *Belleisle*, *Agamemnon* and *Africa* had joined us.

"Towards the close of the evening of the 20th the Admiral (by telegraph) told Captain Blackwood he firmly relied on his keeping sight of the enemy during the night. The several captains of the lookout ships were on board the *Victory*, and received instructions relative to their conduct, and to inform the Admiral of the enemy's manoeuvres until daylight. His Lordship's instructions were strictly observed, and every movement of the enemy was indicated to us by our chain of communication, and as the enemy tacked or wore we had immediate intelligence of it, and regulated our conduct accordingly . . .

"Various reports had gained our ears [as to the reason] for their coming out of port. Scarcity of provisions were among the most prevalent. But, whatever may have been the cause of their temerity, they appeared to seek the action with as much confidence as ourselves (80)."

5 The Day of Trafalgar

"AS THE DAY began to dawn, a man at the topmost head called out, 'A sail on the starboard bow!' And in two or three minutes more he gave another call, that there was more than one sail . . . Indeed they looked like a forest of masts rising from the ocean . . . As morning got light we could plainly discern them from the deck, and were satisfied it was the enemy, for the Admiral began to telegraph to that effect. They saw us, and would gladly have got away when they discovered we counted 27 sail of the line. But it was too late, and situated as they were, hemmed in by Cape Trafalgar on the one side, and not being able to get back to Cadiz on the other (81)."

Tense and alert, the British fleet awaited their enemy. Nelson scribbled a note to Lady Hamilton: ". . . The signal has been made that the enemy's combined fleet are coming out of port. We have very little wind, so that I have no hopes of seeing them before tomorrow. May the God of battle crown my endeavours with success. At all events, I will take care that my name shall ever be most dear to you and Horatia, both of whom I love as much as my own life . . . (82)."

He hurriedly wrote another note to Emma next day, Sunday: "October 20th. In the morning, we were close to the mouth of the Straits [of Gibraltar], but the wind had not come far enough to the westward to allow the combined fleets to weather the shoals off Trafalgar. But they were counted as far as forty sail of ships of war, which I suppose to be thirty-four of the line, and six frigates. A group of them was seen off the lighthouse of Cadiz this morning, but it blows so very fresh and thick weather, that I rather believe they will go into the habour before night. May God Almighty give us success over these fellows, and enable us to get a peace (83)."

Nelson's
instructions
Anxiously, Nelson repeated to Captain Blackwood of the frigate *Euryalus* to keep the enemy in sight of his frigates until the fleet was in battle formation: "Captain Blackwood to keep with two frigates in sight of the Enemy in the night. Two other frigates to be placed between him and the *Defence*, Captain Hope. *Colossus* will take her station between *Defence* and *Mars*. *Mars* to communicate with the *Victory*. Signals by night: If the enemy are standing to the southward, or towards the Straits, burn two blue lights together, every hour, in order to make the greater blaze. If the enemy are standing to the westward three guns, quick, every hour (84)."

Enemy
discovered
At dawn on Monday, 21st October, an officer of the *Belleisle* remembered: "The whole force of the enemy was discovered standing to the southward distant about nine miles, between us and the coast near Trafalgar. I was awakened by the cheers of the crew and by their rushing up the hatchways to get a glimpse of the hostile fleet (85)."

Minutes before six o'clock, Midshipman Badcock on duty watch on the *Neptune*, recalled: "At the first dawn of day a forest of strange masts was seen to leeward. I ran aft and informed the officer of the watch. The Captain was on deck in a moment ... (86)"

Aboard the *Royal Sovereign*, Vice-Admiral Collingwood was dressing with the help of his servant, Smith. "During all this time [he] was shaving himself with a composure that quite astonished me. Admiral Collingwood dressed himself that morning with peculiar care ... meeting Lieutenant Clavell, 'You had better,' he said, 'put on silk stockings, as I have done: for if one should get a shot in the leg, they would be so much more manageable for the surgeon.' (87)"

Battle
signals
Within minutes of sighting the enemy, the *Victory* made signal No. 72 to the fleet: "Form the order of sailing in two columns". Scattered after a night without lights, the fleet began to close up in two lines of battle. The *Victory's* flags were run down, then signal No. 76 went up: "Bear up and sail in direction shown," together with E.N.E. flags. Frigates repeated the signals to outlying ships. Slowly, their yards braced to a new set, their sails filled in the breeze, and the great ships, rolling on the swell, headed round to the

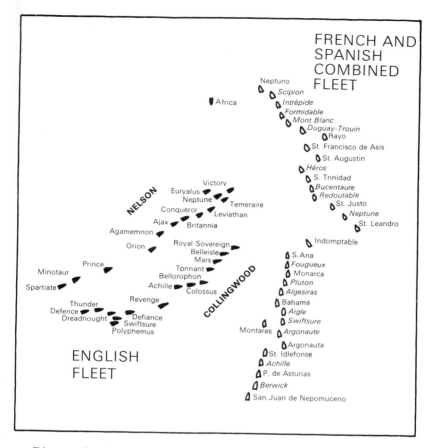

Neptuno
Scipion
Intrépide
Formidable
Mont Blanc
Duguay-Trouin
Rayo
St. Francisco de Asis
St. Augustin
Héros
S. Trinidad
Bucentaure
Redoutable
St. Justo
Neptune
St. Leandro
Indomptable
S. Ana
Fougueux
Monarca
Pluton
Algesiras
Bahama
Aigle
Swiftsure
Argonaute
Argonauta
St. Idlefonse
Achille
P. de Asturias
Berwick
San Juan de Nepomuceno
Montares

Africa

NELSON

Victory
Euryalus
Neptune
Conqueror   Temeraire
Ajax   Leviathan
Agamemnon   Britannia
Orion
Royal Sovereign
Belleisle
Mars
Prince   Tonnant
Minotaur   Bellorophon
Achille
Spartiate   Colossus
Revenge
Thunder
Defence   Defiance
Dreadnought   Swiftsure
Polyphemus

COLLINGWOOD

ENGLISH
FLEET

Diagram showing Nelson's plan of attack using two columns of ships, one led by himself and the other by Collingwood. The diagram shows the position at noon as the first ship came under fire

eastward. The light grew clearer. From the decks the sailors could make out the French and Spanish fleet, scattered for five miles across the horizon, nine or ten miles away.

Throughout the night Villeneuve and Gravina, the French and Spanish Admirals, expected an attack. The British flares and gun fire were never far away. As the darkness lifted, the French and Spanish anxiously scanned the horizon for their enemy. At 6.30 a.m. the frigate *Hermione* flew the warning-signal: "Enemy in sight to windward." No shred of doubt remained: battle was now certain. The whole combined fleet had cleared it decks for action during the night. Nine miles to the west the *Victory* flew its third signal of the

Just before the battle. Officer: "Why Jack, how is this at prayers when the enemy is bearing down upon us. Are you afraid of them?" Jack: "Afraid! No! I was only praying that the Enemy's shot may be distributed in the same proportion as the prize money-the greatest part among the officers."

day, No. 13: "Prepare for battle."

Preparation for battle

William Beatty was surgeon aboard the *Victory*. He wrote later: "His Lordship [Nelson] came upon deck soon after daylight. He was dressed as usual in his Admiral's frock-coat, bearing on the left breast four stars of different orders, which he always wore with his common apparel. He displayed excellent spirits, and expressed his pleasure at the prospect of giving a fatal blow to the naval power of France and Spain . . ." He did not wear his sword: "It had been taken from where it hung up in his cabin, and was laid ready on his table; but he forgot to call for it. This was the only action in which he ever appeared without a sword (88)."

Frantic preparations were taking place aboard every British ship: Second Lieutenant Ellis of the Marines, aboard the *Ajax*,

The gun deck of a typical English ship of the line

recalled that, shortly before seven o'clock, "I was sent below with orders, and was much struck with the preparations made by the blue-jackets, most of whom were stripped to the waist. A handkerchief was tightly bound round their heads and over the ears, to deaden the noise of the cannon, many men being deaf for days after an action . . . Some were sharpening their cutlasses, others polishing the guns . . . whilst three or four, as if in a mere bravado, were dancing a hornpipe. But all seemed anxious to come to close quarters with the enemy. Occasionally they would look out of the ports, and speculate as to the various ships of the enemy, many of whom had been on former occasions engaged by our vessels (89)."

"During this time," recalled Jack Nastyface, "each ship was making the usual preparations, such as breaking away the captain's and officer's cabins, and sending all the lumber below. The doctors, parson, purser and loblolly men [medical aides] were also busy getting the medicine chests and bandages out, and sails prepared for the wounded to be placed on, that they might be dressed in rotation as they were taken down to the aft-cockpit.

"In such a bustling and, it may be said, trying as well as serious time, it is curious to notice the different dispositions of the British sailor. Some would be offering a guinea for a glass of grog, whilst others were making a kind of mutual verbal will, such as: 'If one of Johnny Crapeau's shots (a term given to the French) knocks my head off, you will take all my effects, and if you are killed and I am not, why, I will have yours,' and this is generally agreed to (90)."

Action stations

"On every ship drummers beat to quarters. In the dim light of the gun-decks, gun-crews of 10, 12 or 15 men each begin work. Port-lids are raised and the iron guns, weighing up to $2\frac{1}{2}$ tons, are run forward on massive wooden carriages to the ports. Tompions are taken from muzzles, and breeching ropes anchored to take the recoil. One gun broken loose in action can kill as many men, as it careers across the deck, as enemy gun-fire.

"Tables are stowed, sleeping-hammocks stuffed in the bulwarks for protection against musket-fire. To lessen fire risk, buckets of water are placed ready to wet the canvas screens around hatchways. The decks are sprinkled well with sand to stop them becoming too slippery with blood. Master gunners unlock the powder-magazines and weigh the charge bags. A 32-lb. shot takes a third of its weight in powder. Cannon balls are carried to the guns in hammocks. On the forecastles and poops canisters of musket balls and scrap iron stand by the 68-pounder carronades. The slow-match, for lighting a fuse should a flintlock fail, is lit and burns over a water barrel (91)."

Nelson's diary

Alone in his cabin, Nelson wrote the last entries in his private diary: "At daylight saw the enemy's combined fleet from East to E.S.E. Bore away. Made the signal for Order of Sailing, and to Prepare for Battle; the enemy with their heads to the southward; at seven the enemy wearing in succession. May the Great God, whom I worship, grant to my country, and for the benefit of Europe in general, a great and glorious victory; and may no misconduct in any one tarnish it; and may humanity after victory be the predominant feature in the British fleet. For myself, individually, I commit my life to Him, who made me, and may his blessing light upon my endeavours for serving my country faithfully. To him I resign myself and the just cause which is entrusted to me to defend. Amen. Amen. Amen (92)."

With a foreboding of his own death, he added a codicil to his will. *Nelson's will* He was anxious for the future of Emma and Horatia, and called upon England to provide for them after he had gone. "I leave Emma Lady Hamilton . . . a legacy to my King and country, that they will give her an ample provision to maintain her rank in life. I also leave to the beneficence of my country my adopted daughter, Horatia Nelson Thompson; and I desire she will use in future the name of Nelson only. These are the only favours I ask of my King and country at this moment when I am going to fight their battle. May God bless my King and country, and all those who I hold dear. My relations it is needless to mention: they will of course be amply provided for. Witnessed – Henry Blackwood, T. M. Hardy (93)."

A ship whose rigging was torn down in battle would be unable to move. Jack Nastyface told how the rigging was wrapped up in protective blankets: "The seamen's hammocks with the bedding and blankets were lashed to the shrouds, which served much to save our rigging, as was very evident from examination on the second night after the battle. For when our men got their hammocks down, many were found to have received a great deal of damage, being very much cut with the large shot, and some were found to have had grape or canister shot lodged in them (94)."

Nelson ordered all the British ships to be painted before the *Ships* battle: "It has been a favourite mode with Lord Nelson to paint the *painted* side of all ships under his command in chequers, which made them to be distinguished with greater certainty in case of falling in with an enemy; and became a well known and general term in a squadron or fleet, so much so that, when speaking to any other ship, it was usual to say, 'Oh! she's one of Nelson's chequer-players,' signifying thereby that she had been one of the fighting ships. The seamen . . . took great pride in being considered a chequer player, and could not wish to part with the name (95)."

Unable to slip back into the safety of Cadiz harbour, Villeneuve and Gravina prepared for battle: "As the enemy was thus driven to

67

risk a battle, he exhibited a specimen of their naval tactics by forming themselves into a crescent, or half-moon, waiting for our approach. This did not take place until ten minutes of twelve o'clock, so that there was nearly six hours to prepare for battle . . . We glided down to them under the influence of a gentle breeze, cheering to every seaman's heart, that Providence took us in tow . . . From a signal made by Lord Nelson, our ships were soon formed into two lines, weather and lee (96)." These lines, one led by Nelson in the *Victory*, the other by Collingwood in the *Royal Sovereign*, were to be the bones of Nelson's daring battle plan.

Captain Moorsom of the *Revenge* recalled: "We kept going down in two columns pointing to their centre. All our ships were carrying studding sails, and many bad sailors a long way astern, but little or no stop was made for them (97)."

Nelson's plan of attack at Trafalgar was explained by a lieutenant aboard the *Victory* in a letter to his parents in England: Lord Nelson "determined so to place his fleet that a drawn battle or partial action should be entirely out of the question. Admiral Collingwood and himself led their separate divisions, well knowing that a British seaman will always follow and support his leader. This plan of attack was grand beyond example, and worthy of the great mind that formed it . . .

"It has been usual when two hostile fleets have been in sight of each other to form in line of battle; that is, to place the fleets parallel to each other. Consequently, two fleets of [an] equal number of ships would have a marked opponent (98)."

This line of conduct had always caused great delay: "Fleets have sometimes been in sight of each other for two or three days without being able so completely to form as to risk an action. But by his Lordship's mode of attack you will clearly perceive not an instant of time could be lost; the action would commence as soon as we could arrive up with the enemy. His Lordship's superior arrangement left nothing to be done by signals. The frequent communications he had with his admirals and captains put them in possession of all his plans, so that his mode of attack was well known to every officer of the fleet (99)."

About eight o'clock, the winds were light. The opposing fleets now lay only seven miles apart, their lines still forming. At 8.20

TRAFALGAR TIMETABLE

5.50 a.m.	Combined fleet sighted ten miles away.
6.00 a.m.	Nelson signals fleet to form two columns.
6.30 a.m.	Nelson signals "Prepare for battle."
7.00 a.m.	Villeneuve signals combined fleet to form line of battle.
8.00 a.m.	Fleets seven miles apart. Nelson holds conference with frigate captains, urging them not to let the enemy slip out of sight.
8.45 a.m.	Nelson signals fleet: "Make more sail."
9.20 a.m.	Nelson signals fleet: "Make more sail."
9.40 a.m.	Nelson signals fleet: "Make more sail."
10.00 a.m.	Nelson refuses to leave the *Victory* for *Euryalus*.
10.40 a.m.	Fleets two miles apart. Very light winds.
11.45 a.m.	Fleets 1½ miles apart.
11.50 a.m.	Villeneuve signals combined fleet to open fire as soon as British within range. Nelson signals: "England expects that every man will do his duty."
12.00 p.m.	*Royal Sovereign* goes under fire.
12.10 p.m.	*Royal Sovereign* fires broadside at *Santa Ana* at point blank range.
12.30 p.m.	First broadsides strike the *Victory*, still a mile from the enemy.
1.00 p.m.	The *Victory* engages the *Bucentaure*.
1.15 p.m.	Nelson struck in the shoulder by a musket ball.
1.30 p.m.	*Victory* crashes into the *Redoutable*, and then the *Téméraire*.
2.05 p.m.	Villeneuve surrenders the *Bucentaure*.
2.30 p.m.	Lucas surrenders *Redoutable* to *Victory*.
4.30 p.m.	Death of Nelson.
4.45 p.m.	Gravina in the *Principe de Asturias* leads the flight back to Cadiz.
5.10 p.m.	The *Intrepide* is the last French ship to surrender.
5.15 p.m.	Surrender of the *Neptuno* (Dumanoir).
5.20 p.m.	The last shots of battle are fired.
5.50 p.m.	The *Achille* explodes and capsizes.
6.00 p.m.	Admiral Collingwood makes the *Euryalus* his flagship.

the French and Spanish fleet was signalled to wear. Villeneuve said:
"The enemy's fleet . . . seemed to be heading *en masse* for my rear
squadron, with the double object, apparently, of engaging in
greatly superior force and of cutting the combined fleet off from
Cadiz. I therefore signalled for the fleet to wear all together, and
form line of battle in reverse order (100)."

The proud Villeneuve knew the odds were against him. He was
beset by difficulties. From the start, he had impossible orders from
Napoleon; inexperienced captains, raw sailors, untrained gunners.
He had a fleet which could form a line of battle and little else. He
could not forget the disaster of the Battle of the Nile, when Nelson
had annihilated a great French fleet at Aboukir Bay, seven years
before.

Spaniards'
seamanship
The Spaniards had a poor reputation for seamanship. Jack
Nastyface noted how the combined fleet co-operated: "As we
drew near, we discovered the enemy line was formed with a
Spanish ship between two French ones nearly all through their line,
as I suppose, to make them fight better; and it must be admitted
that the Dons fought as well as the French in that battle; and, if
praise was due for seamanship and valour, they were well entitled
to an equal share (101)."

"Royal
Sovereign"
Jack Nastyface "now began to hear the enemy's cannon opening
on the *Royal Sovereign*, commanded by Lord Collingwood, who
commenced the action . . . A signal being made by the Admiral
to some of our senior captains, to break the enemy's line at different
points, it fell to our lot to cut off the five sternmost ships . . . While
we were running down to them, of course we were favoured with
several shots, and some of our men were wounded.

"Upon being thus pressed, many of our men thought it hard
that the firing should all be on one side, and became impatient to
return the compliment. But our captain had given orders not to
fire until we got close in with them, so that all our shot might tell.
Indeed, these were his words: 'We shall want all our shot when we
get close in. Never mind their firing: when I fire a carronade from
the quarter deck, that will be the signal for you to begin, and I know
you will do your duty as Englishmen (102).'"

"Revenge"
70
Soon, Jack and the *Revenge* were in the thick of the opening
battle. "In a few minutes the gun was fired and our ship bore in

and broke the line. But we paid dear for our temerity . . . Those ships we had thrown into disorder turned round and made an attempt to board. A Spanish three-decker ran her bowsprit over our poop, with a number of her crew in it, and in her fore-rigging two or three hundred men were ready to follow. But they caught a tartar, for their design was discovered and our marines with their small arms, and carronades on the poop, loaded with canister shot, swept them off so fast – some into the water and some on the decks – that they were glad to sheer off.

"While this was going on aft, we were engaged with a French two-deck ship on our starboard side, and on our larboard bow another . . . Many of their shots must have struck their own ships, and done severe execution. After being engaged about an hour, two other ships fortunately came up, received some of the fire intended for us . . . We were now enabled to get at some of the shot-holes between wind and water and plug them up. This is a duty performed by the carpenter and his crew (103)."

As the *Victory's* line of ships approached the enemy line, his officers were worried for Nelson's safety. At about 10 o'clock Dr. Beatty "made known to Dr. Scott his fears that his Lordship would be made the object of the enemy's marksmen, and his desire that he might be entreated by somebody to cover the stars on his coat with a handkerchief (104)." But no one dared to suggest this, and nothing was said. *Concern for Nelson*

"About 10 o'clock," said Blackwood later, "Lord Nelson's anxiety to close with the enemy became very apparent. He frequently remarked that they put a good face upon it; but always quickly added, 'I'll give them such a dressing as they never had before' . . . I proposed hoisting his Flag in the *Euryalus*, whence he could better see what was going on . . . But he would not hear of it, and gave as his reason the force of example (105)."

Blackwood and Hardy, still thinking of Nelson's safety, then suggested that the *Victory* should keep her battle order and let other ships lead the division. Nelson "at length consented to allow the *Téméraire*, which was then sailing abreast of the *Victory*, to go ahead, and hailed Captain Harvey . . . Captain Harvey being rather out of hail, his Lordship sent me to communicate his wishes, which I did. But on returning . . . I found him doing all he could to increase rather than diminish sail, so that the *Téméraire* could not pass . . . (106)."

*Enemy
ships*
By half past ten, the fleets were only two and a half miles apart. Hulls could be seen. Midshipman Badcock said: "Some of the enemy's ships were painted like ourselves – with double yellow sides, some with a broad single red or yellow streak, others all black, and the noble *Santissima Trinidada*, 138 guns, with four distinct lines of red (107)."

Aboard the French *Redoutable*, Captain Jean Lucas had crack marines ready to board the enemy. "I had cartridge-cases made for each of the captains of the guns, to hold two grenades apiece . . . I had a hundred muskets, fitted with long bayonets . . . The picked men to whom these were served out were specially trained at musketry and stationed in the shrouds. All the men with cutlasses and pistols were regularly trained (108)."

Preceded by fifes and drums, the captains of the combined fleet, together with their first officers, inspected the batteries and the gunners, Admiral Villeneuve himself toured the decks of his great flagship, the *Bucentaure*. Everywhere could be heard the sound of drums, cheers, and cries of "Vive l'Empereur! (109)"

Silence
Lt. Hoffman of the *Tonnant* said: "All our ships that had bands were playing *Rule Britannia, Downfall of Paris, etc.* Our own struck up *Britons Strike Home* (110)." But mostly there was silence on the British ships. Midshipman Robinson on the *Euryalus* recalled, "The fleet held steadfastly on its course in grim silence that was unbroken save for, now in one ship, now in another, a gruff, hoarse-toned order, short and sharp, or the chirp of a bo'sun's whistle, the creaking of a spar, or flap of a sail (111)."

Aboard the *Victory*, Badcock saw the enemy sailing into their line of battle: "It was a beautiful sight when their line was completed: their broadsides turned towards us showing their iron teeth . . . In our fleet Union Jacks and ensigns were made fast to the fore and foretopmast-stays, as well as to the mizzen rigging, besides one at the peak, in order that we might not mistake each other in the smoke . . . Nelson had ordered the iron mast-hoops on all British ships to be whitewashed so that, should flags be shot away, the British can still be distinguished from the enemy, whose hoops are black (112)."

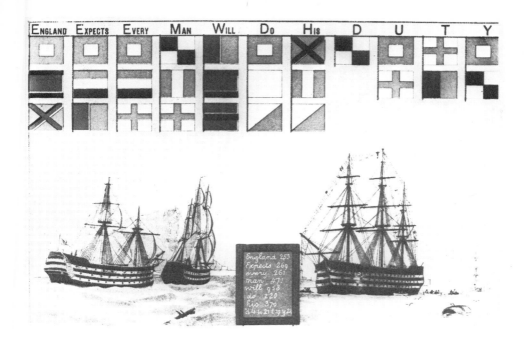

ENGLAND EXPECTS EVERY MAN WILL DO HIS D U T Y

The flags with which Nelson signalled to the fleet, "England expects every man will do his duty"

In the last moments before battle, Nelson decided to make a signal to the fleet: "Nelson confides that every man will do his duty." Blackwood and Hardy suggested that the word "England" would be better than "Nelson". Nelson at once agreed.

Nelson's signal

Flag-Lieutenant Pasco was in charge of signals aboard the *Victory*: "His Lordship came to me on the poop and ... said: 'Mr. Pasco, I want to say to the fleet, *England confides that every man will do his duty*.' He added, 'You must be quick, for I have one more to add, which is for *Close Action!*'" Pasco looked in Sir Home Popham's new signal code issued six weeks before to the battle squadrons. He told Nelson that "confides" would need spelling, letter by letter, whereas "expects" was in the code. Nelson hastily agreed to the second change. "That will do, Pasco; make it directly (113)."

Signalman John Roome, a young Thames bargehand press-ganged into the *Victory* two years before, began tying the signal flags. Pasco said: "As the last hoist was hauled down, Nelson turned to Captain Blackwood ... with, 'Now I can do no more.

Close action

73

EXTRACT FROM NAVAL SIGNALS BOOK

238	Each	1238	Either-wise
239	Early	1239	Eligible
240	East-erly-ward	1240	Else-where
241	East-Indies-an	1241	Embay-ed
243	Ease-y-ily	1243	Employ-ed-ing-er-ment
244	Effect-ed-ing	1244	Empty-iness
245	Embark-ation-ed-ing	1245	Enable-d-ing
246	Encamp-ed-ing-ment	1246	Encourage-d-ing-ment
247	End-ing-less	1247	Endanger-ed-ing
248	Endeavour-ed-ing	1248	Enough
249	Enemy-ies	1249	Entirely
250	Enforce-d-ing	1250	Error-oneous-ly
251	Engage-d-ing-ment	1251	Especial-ly
253	England-ish	1253	Esteem-imate-ion
254	Enjoin-ed-ing	1254	Evacuate-d-ing-ion
255	Entitle-d-ing	1255	Even
256	Enter-ry-ance	1256	Evolution-s
257	Erase-d-ing-ment	1257	Evidence-t-ly
258	Essential-ly	1258	Exact-ly-ness
259	Establish-ed-ing-ment	1259	Excellent-ce-cy-tly
260	Evening	1260	Exceed-ed-ing-ly, excess-ive-ly
261	Ever-y-thing-where		*(sic)*
263	Examine-ation-ed-ing	1261	Except-ed-ing-ion-able
264	Example	1263	Exclude-d-ing-sive-ion
265	Exceed-ed-ing	1264	Expend-ed-ing-ce
266	Excuse-d-ing-able	1265	Explain-ed-ing-ation
267	Execute-d-ing-ion	1266	Explode-sion
268	Exert-ed-ing-ion	1267	Extend-ed-ing-sive-ion
269	Expect-ed-ing-ation	1268	External-ly
270	Expedite-ed-ing-ion-ious	1269	Extinguish-tinct
271	Express-ed-ing-ion-ly	1270	Extol-led-ing
273	Extra-ordinary-ly	1271	Extreme
		1273	Extricate-ed-ing

We must trust to the great Disposer of all events . . .' When Lord Nelson's message had been answered . . . he ordered me to make the signal for Close Action and keep it up. Accordingly I hoisted No. 16 at the top-gallant masthead, and there it remained until shot away (114)."

The *Royal Sovereign*, under full sail, was nearly a mile ahead of the rest of the fleet and almost within range of enemy guns. Impassively, Collingwood chewed an apple as he walked the quarter-deck. His crack gun teams lay on their stomachs, waiting.

England The signal lieutenant began writing numbers on his slate. The
74 *expects . . .* *Victory* was telegraphing the fleet: 253, 269, 863, 261, 471, 958, 220,

370, 4, 21, 19, 24. Collingwood was in no mood for messages: "I wish Nelson would stop signalling; we all know what we have to do." The numbers were deciphered and the signal was read out: "England expects that every man will do his duty." Frigates repeated the signal to the outlying ships. It was noted in ships' logs; on some ships it was read out to the men. Some were puzzled; then cheers sounded across the water.

Within ten minutes, the *Royal Sovereign* came under enemy fire, as a massive broadside exploded from the 74-gun French ship *Fougueux*. Cannon balls screamed through the air and fell into the sea nearby. Within minutes more, the *Royal Sovereign* was crossing under the stern of the great *Santa Ana*, the 112-gun flagship of the Spanish Admiral de Alva. Collingwood ordered a thunderous 50-gun broadside into the *Santa Ana*'s stern. More than 200 Spaniards were killed or wounded, and fourteen guns were put out of action. A thick pall of gun smoke hung on the air, obscuring the deadly conflict of broadside and counter-broadside. *"Royal Sovereign"*

Collingwood wrote in his journal later, "About noon, the *Royal Sovereign* opened a fire on the 12th, 13th, 14th and 15th ships from the enemy's rear, and stood on with all sail to break the enemy's line. A quarter past 12: altered course to port, and in passing close under the stern of the *Santa Ana*, a Spanish three-deck ship with a Vice-Admiral's flag, raked her, and sheering up on her starboard quarter began a very close action. At this time, the *Mars, Tonnant* and *Belleisle* had just broke through the enemy's line and were beginning to engage warmly. The smoke soon became so thick that more of the management of other ships could not be distinguished (115)."

The action quickly became general. At 12.30 the first enemy shots reached the *Victory*, from a mile away. At 1 p.m. the *Victory* crashed into Villeneuve's *Bucentaure*, and came under heavy fire from the *Redoutable* of Captain Lucas. *"Victory"*

Several ships in both fleets were quickly disabled by the heavy broadsides and devastating short-range carronades. Unable to move in the sea they had to attack and defend themselves as best they could: "We were now unable to work the ship, our yards, sails, and masts being disabled, and the braces completely shot away. In this condition we lay by the side of the enemy, firing away, and now

75

Overleaf Admiral Nelson struck by a musket ball in the shoulder fifteen minutes after the *Victory* collided with the *Bucentaure*

and then we received a good raking from them passing under our stern.

"This was a busy time with us, for we had not only to endeavour to repair our damage, but also to keep to our duty. Often during the battle we could not see for the smoke whether we were firing at a foe or a friend, and as to hearing, the noise of the guns had so completely made us deaf, that we were obliged to look only to the motions that were made (116)."

Captain
Lucas
It was the *Redoutable*'s fire that quickly led to Nelson's death. Captain Lucas wrote later: "At last the *Victory's* batteries were not able to reply to us, I perceived that they were preparing to board; the foe thronged up on to their upper works. I ordered the trumpet to sound; it was the recognized signal to summon the boarding parties in our exercises. They came up in such perfect order, with the officers and midshipmen at the head of their divisions, that one would have said that it was only a sham fight. In less than a minute the upper works were covered with armed men who hurled themselves on to the poop, on the nettings and into the shrouds; it was impossible for me to pick out the most courageous.

"Then there began a furious musketry fire in which Admiral Nelson was fighting at the head of his crew. Our fire became so greatly superior, that in less than fifteen minutes we had silenced that of the *Victory*. More than 200 grenades were thrown aboard her with the most marked success. Her upper works were strewn with the dead and wounded, and Admiral Nelson was killed by the fire of our musketry (117)" – at a range of only fifteen yards.

"Almost immediately," Lucas went on, "the upper works of the enemy ship were deserted and the *Victory* ceased absolutely to engage us. But it was difficult to get aboard her owing to the rolling of the two ships, and to the superior height afforded by her third deck (118)."

Fire
At 1.30 p.m. marine Lieutenant Rotely remembered on the *Victory*: "There was the fire from above, the fire from below, besides the fire from the deck I was upon, the guns recoiling with violence, reports louder than thunder, the decks heaving and the sides straining. I fancied myself in the infernal regions . . . Lips might move, but orders and hearing were out of the question; everything was done by signs (119)."

Lucas went on: "I gave orders to cut away the slings of the main-yard and to lower it to serve as a bridge. Midshipman Yon and four seamen succeeded in getting on board the *Victory* by means of the anchor, and informed us that there was not a soul on her decks. But at the moment when our brave lads were just hurling themselves after then the three-decker *Téméraire* – who had doubtless perceived that the *Victory* had ceased fire and would inevitably be taken – ran foul of us to starboard, and overwhelmed us with the point-blank fire of all her guns (120)."

In agony from his shoulder wound, Nelson was quickly carried down below decks by Dr. Beatty and a helper. A handkerchief was thrown over Nelson's face to try and prevent the crew of the *Victory* seeing what had happened to their commander so soon in the battle.

Nelson shot

"Who is that carrying me?" whispered Nelson.

"Beatty, my Lord, and Burke."

"Ah, Mr. Beatty! – you can do nothing for me. I have but a short time to live: my back is shot through."

With a sinking heart, Beatty felt Nelson's blood-soaked coat: "I hope the wound is not as dangerous as your Lordship imagines." They laid Nelson on a mattress against the ship's side, and took off his clothes to examine the wound. Nelson whispered, "I have to leave Lady Hamilton, and my adopted daughter Horatia, as a legacy to my country."

Beatty prepared his surgical instruments, assuring Nelson he would not hurt him too much in trying to find the musket ball. The more Beatty gently probed the more he saw everything was hopeless. The ball had penetrated the chest and lung, and was probably lodged in the spine. He bent over Nelson and explained this to him. "I am confident my back is shot through," said Nelson.

"Tell me all your sensations, my Lord."

"I feel a gush of blood every minute within my breast. I have no feeling in the lower part of my body . . . breathing is very difficult and gives me very severe pain about the part of the spine I am sure the ball has struck – for I felt it break my back . . ."

Beatty listened in despair. He wrote later: "These symptoms, but more particularly the gush of blood which his Lordship complained of, together with the state of his pulse, indicated to the surgeon

No hope

himself the hopeless situation of the case: but till after the victory was ascertained and announced to his Lordship, the true nature of his wound was concealed by the surgeon from all on board except Captain Hardy, Dr. Scott, Mr. Burke and Messrs. Smith and Westemburg, the Assistant Surgeons (121)."

"Téméraire"
and
"Redoutable"

Meantime, the *Téméraire* gave the *Redoutable* a terrific hammering with her broadsides. Captain Lucas wrote, "Our ship was so riddled that she seemed to be no more than a mass of wreckage. In this state the *Téméraire* hailed us to strike [surrender] and not to prolong a useless resistance. I ordered several soldiers who were near me to answer this summons with musket shots, which was performed with great zeal (122)."

But it was hopeless: "All the stern was absolutely stove in, the rudder stock, the tiller, the two tiller sweeps, the stern-post, the helm port and wing transoms, the transom knees, were in general shot to pieces; the decks were all torn open by the fire of the *Victory* and the *Téméraire*; all the guns were shattered or dismounted by the shots or from these two ships having run us aboard.

"An 18-pounder gun on the main deck and a 36-pounder

Nelson attended by Beatty and the other surgeons in the orlop deck, shortly before his death

carronade on the fo'c'sle having burst, killed and wounded many of our people; the two sides of the ship, all the lids and bars of the ports were utterly cut to pieces; four of our six pumps were shattered as well as all our ladders in general . . . (123)."

Lucas added, "All our decks were covered with dead, buried beneath the debris and the splinters from different parts of the ship. A great number of wounded were killed on the orlop deck. Out of the ship's company of 643 men we had 522 disabled, 300 being killed and 222 wounded . . . In the midst of this horrible carnage the brave lads who had not yet succumbed and those who were wounded, with whom the orlop deck was thronged, still cried, 'Vive l'Empereur! We're not taken yet; is our Captain still alive? (124).'" But Lucas could not hold out any longer. "I only awaited the certain knowledge that the leaks which the ship had sprung were so considerable that it could not be long before she foundered, in order to strike (125)." *Surrender*

Still locked to the *Victory*, Villeneuve signalled for his van ships to come to the aid of the *Bucentaure*. But it was too late. Smashed by endless broadsides, the *Bucentaure* herself was helpless. Half his crew lay dead or wounded. The ship's barge and boats were crushed under fallen spars. Villeneuve could not even leave to hoist his Admiral's flag on another vessel. Just after two o'clock he surrendered to Marine Captain James Atcherley, who told of the horror between the *Bucentaure*'s decks: "The dead, thrown back as they fell, lay along the middle of the decks in heaps, and the shot, passing through these, had frightfully mangled the bodies . . . More than 400 had been killed and wounded, of whom an extra-ordinary proportion had lost their heads (126)." *Too late*

Within the next two hours, most of the British ships reached the centre of battle. The *Belleisle*, behind the *Royal Sovereign*, was surrounded and fired on from all sides for nearly three hours. Below decks, "The smoke accumulated more and more thickly, stagnating . . . so densely as to . . . blot out the men at the guns . . . The guns had to be trained [by] orders passed down from above." Men could only hear "the crash of the shot smashing through the rending timbers, and . . . the hoarse bellowings of the captains of the guns . . . calling out to the survivors, 'Close up there! Close up!' (127)" *Centre of battle*

81

Overleaf "Subtraction"–a cartoonist's view of the effect of a cannon ball on a line of sailors (H. Heath)

Sailors boarding an enemy ship in the thick of the battle

By now 33 officers and men of the *Belleisle* lay dead, with 93 wounded. All three mainmasts with their rigging and sails, the bowsprit, figurehead, boats, and even the anchors were shot away. "We lay a mere hulk, covered in wreck and rolling with the swell . . . At this hour a two-decked ship was seen . . . We had scarcely seen British colours since one o'clock . . . It is impossible to express our emotion as an alteration of the stranger's course displayed the white ensign to our sight (128)."

Another British ship, the *Swiftsure*, passed close by the *Belleisle's* stern. In answer to the *Swiftsure's* cheers some on the *Belleisle* held up a Union Jack tied to a pike, while a white ensign drooped from the stump of the mizen mast. The Captain of the *Belleisle* noted: "Ceased firing, and turned the hands up to clear the wreck. Sent a boat and took possession of the Spanish 80-gun ship, *Argonauta* . . . At 4.15 the *Naiad* came down and took us in tow . . . (129)."

By mid-afternoon the Spanish ships were in disarray. Under attack from the *Defence*, the *San Ildefonso* surrendered at 3.30 p.m. Admiral Gravina's flagship, the *Principe de Asturias*, was now the only ship in his squadron still in the battle. But she was soon overtaken by Captain Grindall in the 98-gun *Prince*, and by several other vessels: *Spanish ships surrender*

"She discharged all her guns at grape-shot range into our stern. Admiral Gravina was wounded in the left leg; he was obliged to go below but while it was being temporarily dressed he gave orders that he should be conveyed back and placed at his post on deck. Weakened by loss of blood he fell fainting; but quickly coming to himself, and not perceiving the national colours, he ordered them to be hoisted without delay and he resumed command. In this critical position we sighted the [French] *Neptune* and the *San Justo* that were coming up to our aid, which was observed by the enemy, who obliged them to sheer off (130)."

The French Captain Infernet, who began his career in the French navy as a cabin boy, told of the suffering of his ship the *Intrépide*. (His times are an hour ahead of those recorded by the British ships): "At four o'clock I was dismantled to such a degree that all my rigging was cut to pieces, and several guns on deck and in the batteries dismounted. At 4.45 I ordered the few hands remaining *French suffering*

85

Overleaf Scene aboard the *Victory* shortly before Nelson's death

on deck to go below to the batteries in order to engage to starboard and larboard; at this minute the mizen-yard where my colours were flying was carried away by a shot. I immediately ordered a flag to be flown from the mizen shrouds to starboard and larboard, and continued the fight.

"At five o'clock the wheel, the tiller-sweep, the tiller ropes and the tiller were shattered to a thousand pieces. I at once had the spare tiller rigged and steered with it, always fighting desperately. At 5.15 the mizen mast fell; four or five minutes later the mainmast did the same. I still fought – and I am able to say so to the honour of those whom I commanded – undauntedly. I was then surrounded by seven enemy ships, which were all firing into me and I was making all possible resistance. I was firing with the stern-chasers, musketry from the upper-works and from the fore-tops (131)."

A young French marquis aboard the *Intrépide* was in charge of the sharpshooters, and the boarders. Amid the smoke and noise of the guns, "What took much of my attention was to prevent the masts and yards from coming down, and I was able to keep the foremast standing for a considerable time, by means of which we were able to manoeuvre the ship to some extent.

"While the fighting was very hot the British *Orion* crossed our bows in order to pour in a raking fire. I got my men ready to board and pointing out to a midshipman her position and what I wanted to do, I sent him to the Captain with a request to have the ship laid on board the *Orion*.

"I saw to the rest, and seeing the ardour of my men, I already imagined myself master of the British seventy-four and taking her into Cadiz with her colours under ours. With keen anxiety I waited; but there was no change in the *Intrépide*'s course.

"Then I dashed off to the quarter-deck myself. On the way I found my midshipman lying flat on the deck, terrified at the sight of the *Britannia*, which ship had come abreast of us within pistol shot and was thundering into us from her lofty batteries. I treated my emissary as he deserved – I gave him a hearty kick – and then I hurried aft to explain my project personally to the Captain. It was then, though, too late. The *Orion* swept forward across our bows, letting fly a murderous broadside – and no second chance presented itself.

"At the moment I reached the poop the brave Infernet was brandishing a small curved sabre which struck off one of the pieces of wooden ornamental work by the rail. The sword blade went close to my face, and I said laughingly, 'Do you want to cut my head off, Captain?'

"'No, certainly not you, my friend,' was the reply, 'but that's what I mean to do to the first man who speaks to me of surrender.'

"Nearby was a gallant colonel of infantry, who had distinguished himself at Marengo. He was terribly perturbed at the broadside from the *Britannia*. In vain he tried to dodge and shelter behind the stalwart form of the Captain, who at length saw what he was doing.

"'Ah, Colonel,' called out the Captain, 'do you think I am sheathed in metal then?' In spite of the gravity of the moment we could not keep from laughing.

"But by now, indeed, the decks had been almost swept clear, our guns were disabled, and the batteries heaped up with dead and dying. It was impossible to keep up a resistance which meant the doom of what remained of our brave ship's company, and ourselves, without the means of striking back and inflicting harm on the enemy (132)."

Captain Infernet takes up the story again: "At 5.53 p.m. the foremast fell; I was then left without masts or sails. Seeing myself surrounded by enemies and not being able to escape, having, moreover, no French ships in sight to come to my assistance, the enemy keeping up a terrible fire into me, having about half my crew killed . . . I was obliged to yield to the seven enemy ships that were engaging me (133)." *Captain Infernet*

Captain Senhouse of the *Conqueror* wrote that the French captain surrendered "after one of the most gallant defences I ever witnessed. The Frenchman's name was Infernet, a member of the Legion of Honour, and it deserves to be recorded in the memory of those who admire true courage (134)."

The *Intrépide* was the last French ship to surrender. Admiral Villeneuve had surrendered his flagship, the *Bucentaure*, three hours before. Five minutes later the Spanish ship *Neptuno* also struck her colours. The handful of enemy ships still afloat and capable of sailing were already limping back to safety in Cadiz. Gravina's

89

Overleaf General view of the Battle of Trafalgar at its height; notice how many sails are shot through

flagship the *Principe de Asturias* was taken in tow by the French *Thémis*.

At half-past four, Nelson still lay, barely living, on the orlop deck of the *Victory*, below the water line. The surgeons raised the end of the sail-cloth mattress, and kept Nelson's shoulders up to ease his agony.

Death of Nelson Dr. Beatty recalled the end: "Lord Nelson now desired . . . his steward to turn him upon his right side; which being effected, his Lordship said: 'I wish I had not left the deck, for I shall soon be gone.'" Nelson "afterwards became very low . . . and his voice faint. He said to Doctor Scott, 'Doctor, I have not been a great sinner,' and after a short pause, 'Remember that I leave Lady Hamilton and my daughter Horatia as a legacy to my country: . . . never forget Horatia.' . . . then, with evident increase of pain . . . pronounced distinctly these last words: 'Thank God, I have done my duty . . .'

"His Lordship became speechless in about fifteen minutes after Captain Hardy left him. When he had remained speechless about five minutes, his . . . steward went to the surgeon. . . . The surgeon . . . knelt down by his side, and took up his hand, which was cold, and the pulse gone from the wrist. On . . . feeling his forehead, which was likewise cold, his Lordship opened his eyes, looked up, and shut them again. The surgeon again left him, and returned to the wounded . . . but was not absent five minutes before the steward announced to him that 'he believed his Lordship had expired.' The surgeon returned, and found that . . . his Lordship had breathed his last, at thirty minutes past four o'clock (135)."

A secret The news of Nelson's death was kept a secret from most of the fleet for another hour or so, until the battle was over. Jack Nastyface explained, "It was shortly made known by one of our boat's crew that Lord Nelson had received a fatal shot; had this news been communicated through the fleet before the conflict was over, what effect it might have had on the hearts of our seamen I know not, for he was adored, and in fighting under him, every man thought himself sure of success; a momentary but naturally melancholy pause among the survivors of our brave crew ensued (136)."

6 Mopping Up

IN THE EVENING DARKNESS, when the battle had died away, there came the dreadful task of clearing the human carnage from the blood-stained decks. "Orders were now given to fetch the dead bodies from the after cockpit and throw them overboard. These were the bodies of men who were taken down to the doctor during the battle, badly wounded and who, by the time the engagement was ended, were dead.

"Some of these perhaps could not have recovered, while others might, had timely assistance been rendered . . . [But] this was impossible, for the rule as to order is requisite, that every person shall be dressed in rotation as they are brought down wounded—and in many instances some have bled to death (137)."

A lieutenant of the *Belleisle* vividly described conditions aboard his ship after the battle. He spoke of one gallant officer who "was severely wounded in the thigh, and underwent an amputation, but . . . he expired before the action had ceased. The junior lieutenant was likewise mortally wounded on the quarter-deck. These gallant fellows were lying beside each other in the gun room preparatory to their being committed to the deep . . . Here many met to take a last look at their departed friends, whose remains soon followed the promiscuous multitude, without distinction of either rank or nation, to their wide ocean grave. In the act of launching a poor sailor over the poop he was discovered to breathe. He was, of course, saved . . .

"The upper deck presented a confused and dreadful appearance. Masts, yards, sails, ropes and fragments of wreck were scattered in every direction. Nothing could be more horrible than the scene of

Horrible spectacle

93

INSTRUMENTS OF A NAVAL SURGEON

2 amputating knives
1 amputating saw with spare blade
1 metacarpal saw with spare blade
2 catlins (double-edged amputating knives)
Pair of artery forceps
2 doz. curved needles
2 tenaculums (hooks for holding parts)
6 Pettit's screw tourniquets
Pair of bone nippers and turnscrew
3 trephines
Saw for the head
Rugins (raspatories or files)
Pair of forceps
Elevator
Brush
2 trocars (tube for withdrawing fluid)
2 silver catheters (tube for drawing off urine)
2 gum elastic catheters
6 scalpels
1 small razor
Key tooth instrument (for extracting teeth by torsion)
Gum lancet (for lancing gum boils)
2 pairs tooth forceps
Punch

2 Seton needles (for drawing silk through the skin to leave a tract for drainage)
Pair of strong probe scissors
Curved bistory with button (scalpel)
Long probe
Pair of bullet forceps
Scoop for extracting balls
2 Probangs (throat sponges)
1 lb. ligature thread
1 paper of needles
Case, with lift-out
Apparatus for restoring suspended animation
Set of pocket instruments
6 lancets in a case
2 pint pewter clyster syringes (enema syringes)
2 sets common splints
Set of Japanned iron splints for legs
12 flannel or linen rollers
2 18-tailed bandages
20 yards of cloth for tourniquets
60 yards of tape
Cupping apparatus, consisting of 1 scarificator and 6 glasses

blood and mangled remains with which every part was covered, and which from the quantity of splinters, resembled a shipwright's yard strewed with gore.

"From our extensive loss – thirty-four killed and ninety-six wounded – our cockpit exhibited a scene of suffering which rarely occurs. I visited this abode of suffering with the natural impulse which led many others thither, namely to ascertain the fate of a friend or companion . . . My nerves were but little accustomed to such trials, but even the dangers of battle did not seem more terrific than the spectacle before me.

Mutilated remains   "On a long table lay several anxiously looking for their turn to receive the surgeon's care, yet dreading the fate he might pronounce. One subject was undergoing amputation, and every part was heaped with sufferers: their piercing shrieks and expiring groans were echoed through this vault of misery . . . Even at this distant period, the heart-sickening picture is alive in my memory. What a contrast to the hilarity and enthusiastic mirth which reigned in this spot the preceding evening! At all other times the cockpit is the region of conviviality and good humour, for here it is that the happy midshipmen reside . . . But a few short hours before on these benches, which were now covered with mutilated remains, sat these scions of their country's glory, who hailed the coming hour of conflict with cheerful confidence. . . .

"About five o'clock the officers assembled in the captain's cabin to take some refreshment. The parching effect of the smoke made this a welcome summons, although some of us had been fortunate in relieving our thirst by plundering the captain's grapes which hung round his cabin . . . There sat a melancholy on the brows of some who mourned a messmate who had shared their perils and their vicissitudes for many years. Then the merits of the departed heroes were repeated with a sigh, but their errors sunk with them into the deep. . . .

Mourning the dead

"A boat with a lieutenant from the cutter *Entreprenante* shortly after came on board, on his return from the *Victory*, to announce the death of the immortal Nelson. The melancholy tidings spread through the ship in an instant, and the paralysing effect was wonderful [*i.e..* amazing].

"Our Captain [Hargood] had served under the illustrious chief for years, and had partaken in the anxious pursuit of the enemy across the Atlantic, with the same officers and crew. 'Lord Nelson is no more!' was repeated with such despondency and heartfelt sorrow, that everyone seemed to mourn a parent. All exertion was suspended. The veteran sailor indulged in silent grief, and some eyes evinced that tenderness of heart which is often concealed under the roughest exterior (138)."

The constant danger of running aground kept the crews sounding the depth of water by lead lines. The frigate *Euryalus*: "At 9.0 sounded in 23 fathoms – made the signal with a gun, Prepare to anchor . . . At 9.15 sounded in 15 fathoms. At 9.20 in 14 fathoms. At 9.35 the water deepened. At 11.0 sounded in 36 fathoms. At 11.20 the water shoaled to 26 fathoms. At 12.0 in 22 fathoms . . . At 12.15 made the signal with three guns to wear, and wore ship – came to the wind on the larboard tack, head to the westward – *Sovereign*

Running aground

95

H.M.S. *Victory* suffered severe damage during the battle

in tow. Fleet and prizes in company (139)."

Repairing the damage
The *Prince* "hauled down fore-topmast staysail to repair shot-holes . . . got fore-runners and tackles forward to secure foremast – cleared away the wreck from the prizes in tow . . . took some Spanish officers on board – came on to blow a hard gale and rain – split the mizen foresail . . . *Trinidada* in tow . . . Strong gales and rain – saw some of the fleet at times, very much mauled, and greatest part partly dismasted (140)."

To revive the men's weakened spirits, tots of rum were issued to

Their masts broken, their sails and rigging shot through, the ships struggle
with the gale that blew up after darkness fell

the crews: "The next call was, 'All hands to splice the main brace!' – which is the giving out a gill of rum to each man . . . Indeed, they much needed it, for they had not ate or drank from breakfast time. We had now a good night's work before us. All our yards, masts, and sails were sadly cut, indeed the whole of the sails were obliged to be unbent, being rendered completely useless, and by the next morning we were partly jury-rigged (141)."

Prizes Captain Moorsom's *Revenge*, like the other ships, began to search for prizes in the smoke-filled evening. "We now began to look for our prizes, as it was coming on to blow hard on the land, and Admiral Collingwood made signals for each ship that was able to take a prize in tow, to prevent them drifting into their own harbour as they were complete wrecks and unmanageable.

"We took an 80-gun Spanish ship in tow for a day and night, but were obliged to cast her off, it blew so hard, and our ship being so very much disabled. Indeed, we were obliged to scuttle a few of them. Some we contrived to take into Gibraltar, some were wrecked near Cadiz harbour, and others drifted into the harbour from whence they had only come two days before. It was a mortifying sight to witness the ships we had fought so hard for, and had taken as prizes, driven by the elements from our possession, with some of our own men on board as prize masters . . . (142)."

The carnage had been terrible aboard the English ships, yet it was worse on the ruined decks of the enemy: "Some of our men were sent on board of the Spanish ship . . . in order to assist at the pumps, for she was much shattered in the hull between wind and water. The slaughter and havoc our guns had made rendered the scene of carnage horrid to behold. There were a number of dead bodies piled up in the hold. Many, in a wounded or mutilated state, were found lying amongst them, and those who were so fortunate as to escape our shot were so dejected and crestfallen that they could not, or would not, work at the pumps, and of course the ship was in a sinking state (143)."

Increasing gale As if this were not enough, "The gale at this time was increasing so rapidly that manning the pumps was of no use, and we were obliged to abandon our prize, taking away with us all our men and as many prisoners as we could. On the last boat's load leaving the ship, the Spaniards who were left on board appeared on the gangway and ship's side, displaying their bags of dollars and doubloons, and eagerly offering them as a reward for saving them from the expected and unavoidable wreck. But however well inclined we were, it was not in our power to rescue them, or it would have been effected without the proffered bribe.

"Here, a very distressing and affecting scene took place . . . A father and his son came down the ship's side to get on board one of our boats. The father had already seated himself, but the men in the boat – thinking from the load and boisterous weather that all their lives would be in peril – could not think of taking the boy. As the boat put off, the lad, as though determined not to quit his father, sprang from the ship into the water, and caught hold of the gunwale of the boat. But his attempt was resisted as it risked all their lives . . . Some of the men resorted to their cutlasses to cut his fingers off, in order to disengage the boat from his grasp. At the same time, the feelings of the father were so worked upon, that he was about to leap overboard and perish with his son.

"Britons could face an enemy, but could not witness such a scene of self-devotion. As it were, a simultaneous thought burst forth from the crew, which said, 'Let us save both the father and son, or die in the attempt.' The Almighty aided them in their design. They succeeded, and brought father and son safe on board our ship where they remained until with other prisoners they were exchanged at Gibraltar (144)."

The *Trinidada*, the largest ship in the world, had suffered terribly. An officer from the *Prince* said: "Our first night's work on board the *Trinidada* was to heave the dead overboard, which amounted to 254 killed (145)." Midshipman Badcock said: "Her beams were covered with blood, brains and pieces of flesh, and the after part of her decks with wounded, some without legs and some without an arm." Another added, "Blood ran in streams about the deck . . . and the rolling of the ship carried it hither and thither until it made strange patterns on the planks (146)."

The wounded were lowered over the stern to be taken off. "We had to tie the poor mangled wretches round their waists, or where we could, and lower them into a tumbling boat, some without arms, others no legs, and lacerated all over . . . (147)"

Captain Robert Moorsom of the *Revenge* told his father of an

Overleaf Hundreds of sailors were swept overboard during the battle, and clung to broken spars praying to be rescued

COMBINED FLEET: CASUALTIES AND DAMAGE

SHIP	KILLED	WOUNDED	FATE
Bucentaure (F)	197	85	Ran ashore, dismasted.
S. Trinidad (Sp)	216	116	Dismasted, Captured and sunk.
Redoutable (F)	490	81	Dismasted, captured and sunk.
Monarca (Sp)	101	154	Captured, ran ashore.
Argonauta (Sp)	100	203	Captured and sunk.
Neptuno (Sp)	38	35	Captured, ran ashore.
Rayo (Sp)	4	14	Went ashore, burnt.
S. Francisco de Asis (Sp)	5	12	Went ashore.
San Augustin (Sp)	184	210	Captured and burnt.
Intrépide (F)	242	not known	Captured and burnt.
Indomptable (F)	Two thirds	not known	Went ashore.
Fougueux (F)	546 killed and wounded		Captured, ran ashore.
Aigle (F)	Two thirds killed and wounded		Captured, ran ashore.
Achille (F)	480 killed and wounded		Blew up.
Berwick (F)	Nearly all drowned		Captured, ran ashore.
Swiftsure (F)	68	123	Captured, taken to Gibraltar.
Bahama (Sp)	75	66	Captured, taken to Gibraltar.
San Ildefonso (Sp)	36	129	Captured, dismasted, taken to Gibraltar.
S. J. Nepomuceno (Sp)	103	151	Captured, taken to Gibraltar.
Formidable (F)	22	45	Captured November 4.
Scipion (F)	17	22	Captured November 4.
Duguay-Trouin (F)	12	24	Captured November 4.
Mont-Blanc (F)	20	20	Captured November 4.
Santa Ana (Sp)	104	137	Recaptured, reached Cadiz, dismasted.
P. de Asturia (Sp)	54	109	Lost main and mizen in gale, reached Cadiz.
Pluton (F)	60	132	Again reached Cadiz, sinking.
Héros (F)	12	24	Reached Cadiz, rigging and rudder damaged.
Neptune (F)	15	39	Again reached Cadiz, undamaged.
Algésiras (F)	77	142	Recaptured, dismasted, reached Cadiz.
Argonaute (F)	55	132	Masts damaged, rudder lost, reached Cadiz.
San Leandro (Sp)	8	22	Masts, hulls damaged. Reached Cadiz.
San Justo (Sp)	—	7	Masts, hulls damaged. Reached Cadiz.
Montanes (Sp)	20	29	Lost foremast, reached Cadiz.

BRITISH FLEET: ORDER OF BATTLE AND SAILING AND CASUALTIES
Van Squadron—Starboard Division

SHIP	GUNS	KILLED	WOUNDED	COMMANDER
Téméraire	98	47	76	Captain Eliab Harvey
Victory	100	57	102*	V-Ad. Lord Nelson; Captain T. M. Hardy
Neptune	98	10	34	Captain Thomas Fremantle
Conqueror	74	3	9	Captain Israel Pellew
Agamemnon	64	2	7	Captain Sir Edward Berry
Leviathan	74	4	22	Captain Henry Bayntun
Ajax	74	2	2	Lt. John Pilfold
Orion	74	1	21	Captain Edward Codrington
Minotaur	74	3	20	Captain C. J. M. Mansfield
Africa	64	18	37	Captain Henry Digby
Spartiate	74	3	17	Captain Sir Francis Laforey, Bt.

Rear Squadron—Port Division

SHIP	GUNS	KILLED	WOUNDED	COMMANDER
Prince	98	—	—	Captain Richard Grindall
Mars	74	29	69	Captain George Duff
R. Sovereign	100	47	94	V-Ad. C. Collingwood; Captain E. Rotheram
Tonnant	80	26	50	Captain Charles Tyler
Belleisle	74	33	93	Captain William Hargood
Bellerophon	74	27	123	Captain J. Cooke
Colossus	74	40	160	Captain James N. Morris
Achille	74	13	59	Captain Richard King
Polyphemus	64	2	4	Captain Robert Redmill
Revenge	74	28	51	Captain Robert Moorsom
Britannia	100	10	40	R-Ad. the Earl of Northesk; Captain C. Bullen
Swiftsure	74	9	8	Captain William Rutherford
Defence	74	7	29	Captain George Hope
Thunderer	98	4	12	Lt. John Stockham
Defiance	74	17	53	Captain Philip Durham
Dreadnought	98	7	26	Captain John Conn

Frigates

SHIP	GUNS	KILLED	WOUNDED	COMMANDER
Euryalus	—	—	—	Captain the Hon Henry Blackwood
Naiad	—	—	—	Captain Thomas Dundas
Phoebe	—	—	—	Captain the Hon Thomas Bladen Capel
Sirius	—	—	—	Captain William Prowse

Schooner

SHIP	GUNS	KILLED	WOUNDED	COMMANDER
Pickle	—	—	—	Lt. John Lapenotiere

Cutter

SHIP	GUNS	KILLED	WOUNDED	COMMANDER
Entreprenante	—	—	—	Lt. Robert Young

*Twenty-seven more men reported wounded after the official return of 75 was made up, according to the *Victory*'s surgeon, Beatty.

Note: The ships did not eventually go into action in this order. The original Order of Battle and Sailing included several other ships which did not arrive in time for the Battle.

incident after the battle, while they were picking up survivors: "I must tell you an anecdote of a Frenchwoman. The *Pickle* schooner sent to me about fifty people saved from the *Achille*, which was burnt and blew up. Amongst them was a young Frenchwoman of about twenty-five, the wife of one of the main topmen. When the *Achille* was burning, she got out of the gunroom port and sat on the rudder-chains till some melted lead ran down upon her and forced her to strip and leap off. She swam to a spar where several men were, but one of them bit and kicked her till she was obliged to quit and get to another which supported her. She was taken up by the *Pickle* and sent on board the *Revenge*, and amongst the men she was lucky enough to find her husband. We were not wanting in civility to the lady. I ordered her two purser's shirts to make a petticoat; and most of the officers found something to clothe her. In a few hours Jeannette was perfectly happy and hard at work on her petticoat . . . (148)."

Next day

On the morrow of the battle, Tuesday, October 22nd, heavy seas and gales dispersed the broken fleets. Everyone was hard at work tending the sick, repairing the damaged vessels, and trying to maintain contact in the difficult conditions. The men of the *Belleisle*, for example: "A.M. – Variously employed. At 8.0, mustered the ship's company by the ship's books. Found killed in battle two lieutenants, one midshipman, and 31 seamen and marines, and 94 seamen and marines wounded. At noon, in tow by the *Naiad*. Part of the fleet in sight.

"P.M. – Strong gales and squally with rain. Set the main and mizen staysails. Employed pumping ship with the chain pumps. At 8.0, thick weather. Fleet not in sight. At 11.0, wore: ship making much water (149)."

The Captain of the *Prince* made a similar report: "A.M. – Made sail to the westward with light winds. At daylight observed nine sail totally dismasted, some in tow of other ships. Hauled down fore topmast staysail to repair shot holes. Set second jib. Found the bowsprit badly wounded and bowsprit shrouds shot away, and part of mainstay. Got fore-runners and tackles forward to secure fore mast. Cleared away the wreck from the prize in tow. Came on to blow hard with rain. Took some Spanish officers on board. Came on a hard gale and rain. Split the mizen topsail, furled fore topsail.

Trinidada in tow. Employed knotting fore and mizen rigging, and securing the masts and securing the tow. Strong gales and rain. Saw some of the fleet at times very much straggled, and greatest part dismasted. Blowing very hard. At noon, employed securing guns and clearing decks, &c. Victualled 145 prisoners. Sun obscure.

"P.M.–Strong gales and squally with rain. Split mizen topsail. In fore topsail. Sailmakers repairing it. Got flying jib boom in. Came onto blow very hard. At 3.30, tow broke adrift. Employed fishing mizen mast and repairing sails. Came on a hard gale. Kept a light for the prize to know our position. Hard gales and rain all night (150)."

An Englishman living in Cadiz found battle wreckage strewn all along the Spanish beaches: "As far as the eye could reach, the sandy side of the isthmus bordering on the Atlantic was covered with masts and yards, the wreckage of ships . . . Among others I noticed a topmast marked with the name of the *Swiftsure*, and the broad arrow of England (151)." *Battle wreckage*

In the weary aftermath of the great battle, the English sailors began to squabble amongst themselves: "Whilst we were at this place [Gibraltar], patching our shattered hulk to make us seaworthy for returning home, some of the crews of the different ships in the fleet would occasionally meet on shore, and one would say to another tauntingly, on enquiring to what ship he belonged, 'Oh! you belong to one of the ships that did not come up till the battle was nearly over!'

"Others would be heard to say, 'Oh! you belong to one of the Boxing Twelves; come and have some black strap and Malaga wine,' at the same time giving them a hearty shake by the hand. This was signifying that the heat of the battle was borne by the twelve ships which first engaged and broke the line.

"And though in a great measure this was true; yet no fault or blame could be attributed either to the officers or men belonging to the ships, as it was the tremendous firing from the ships first engaged, which so becalmed the water and lulled the winds, that a few of our largest ships could only come up in time to receive a straggling shot or two, and take possession of some of the prizes (152)."

After taking in provisions at Gibraltar, the ships made their way

Return home home, and the sailors were granted a well-earned leave. Jack Nastyface was one to receive a six-day "liberty ticket": "Our ship being made seaworthy, we set sail for Old England, and arrived safe at Spithead. The next day we weighed anchor for Portsmouth and on our way into the harbour mouth we were loudly cheered and welcomed home by an immense number of persons who came to greet us on the occasion. The ship being put into dock to repair, the crew were sent on board of a hulk, from which many of them obtained a temporary leave of absence . . .

"I had a six days' liberty ticket, with which, and two shillings and ninepence in my pocket, I was resolved to go to London (153)."

The Rock of Gibraltar, the gateway to the Mediterranean

7 A Great Victory

"GOOD HEAVENS! What news!" wrote one lady on hearing of the victory of Trafalgar. "How glorious if it was not so cruelly damp'd by Nelson's death. How truly he has accomplish'd his prediction that when they meet it must be to extermination. To a man like him he could not have pick'd a finer close to such a life. But what an irreparable loss to England! . . . Do you know, G., it makes me feel almost as much envy as compassion; I think I should like to die so. Think of being mourned by a whole nation, and having my name carried down with gratitude and praise to the latest generations! (154)."

The news of Trafalgar was conveyed in Admiral Collingwood's despatches, sent ashore at Falmouth on 4th November from the frigate *Pickle*. Lieutenant Lapenotière took the despatches by post coach to the Admiralty in London, arriving after a 37-hour journey up from the coast. "Sir!" he told the First Secretary, "We have gained a great victory, but we have lost Lord Nelson!" *A gain and a loss*

Crowds filled the London newspaper offices, shouting for news of their beloved hero, Nelson. "The scene at the Admiralty was quite affecting–crowds of people, chiefly women, enquiring for husbands, brothers, children . . . (155)." As the news of Nelson's death spread, "almost everybody wears a black *crèpe* scarf or cockade with 'Nelson' written on it–this is almost general high and low (156)."

"The Metropolis was very generally and brilliantly illuminated on the occasion, yet there was a damp upon the public spirit, which it was impossible to overcome. Even many of the devices and transparencies indicated that the loss of Lord Nelson was more lamented than the victory was rejoiced at (157)" reported one newspaper.

Illuminations were started but discontinued, "the people being unable to rejoice." "As we came away [from the Admiralty] there was a vast rush of people, but all silent, or a murmur of respect and sorrow; some of the common people saying, 'It is bad news if Nelson is killed,' yet they knew twenty ships had been taken (158)."

The poet Samuel Taylor Coleridge was in Italy when the news came: "Numbers stopped and shook hands with me because they had seen tears on my cheeks and conjectured that I was an Englishman: and some as they held my hand, burst themselves into tears."

Great joy To all old sailors, the news of Trafalgar was a great joy. John Nicol remembered, "When the news of the victory of Trafalgar arrived, I had my triumph over them in return. None but an old tar can feel the joy I felt. I wrought none the next day, but walked about enjoying the feeling of triumph. Every now and then I felt the greatest desire to hurra aloud, and many a hurra my heart gave that my mouth uttered not (159)."

News to home A sailor aboard the *Royal Sovereign* wrote home to his father in Lancashire: "Honoured Father, This comes to tell you that I am alive and hearty, except three fingers – but that's not much, it might have been my head. I told my brother Tom that I should like to see a greadly [great] battle and I have seen one, and we have peppered the combined fleet rarely. And for matter of that, they fought us pretty tightish for French and Spanish. Three of our mess are killed, and four more of us winged. But to tell you the truth of it, when the game began I wished myself at Warnborough with my plough again, but when they had given us one duster, and I found myself snug and tight, I bid fear kiss my bottom and set to in good earnest, and thought no more of being killed than if I were at Murrell Green Fair; and I was presently as busy and as black as a collier.

"How my fingers got knocked overboard I don't know, but off they are and I never missed them till I wanted them. You see by my writing it was my left hand, so I can write to you and fight for my King yet. We have taken a rare parcel of ships, but the wind is so rough we cannot bring them home, else I should roll in money, so we are busy smashing them and blowing 'em up wholesale.

"Our dear Admiral Nelson is killed, so we have paid pretty

THE TIMES
For 7th NOVEMBER. 1805

BATTLE OF
TRAFALGAR

CAPTURE OF
FRENCH AND
SPANISH FLEETS

DEATH OF NELSON
List of Killed and Wounded

Poster announcing the news of Trafalgar in London

sharply for licking 'em. I never set eyes on him, for which I am both sorry and glad. For, to be sure, I should have liked to have seen him – but then all the men in our ship who have seen him are such soft toads they have done nothing but blast their eyes and cry, ever since he was killed. God bless you! Chaps that fought like the Devil, sit down and cry like a wench. I am still in the *Royal Sovereign*, but the Admiral [Collingwood] has left her, for she is like a horse without a bridle, so he is in a frigate that he may be here and there and everywhere, for he's as cute a here-and-there one, and as bold as a lion, for all he can cry! I saw his tears with my own eyes, when the boat hailed and said my Lord was dead. So no more at present from your dutiful son, Sam (160)."

Blockade of France
In the months after Trafalgar, the Royal Navy resumed its blockade of enemy ports for the rest of the war. Trafalgar had destroyed French seapower under Napoleon. Gone were Napoleon's dreams now, of invading England. Instead, England could land her armies and supplies almost anywhere on the continent of Europe, and was now able to begin the long struggle towards victory on land – although the decisive battle of Waterloo was not to be fought until 1815.

Jack Nastyface served in the blockade of Spain: "After refitting, we sailed to join the blockading squadron off Cadiz, and remained there about eighteen months, during which time we were tackling or wearing ship continually, as the blockading service required us to keep as near the harbour's mouth as possible . . . to prevent the escape of the enemy (161)."

The blockade was boring work. But it offered some excitement to the sailors: "We sometimes fired at, and brought to, some of the Spanish fishing boats, and by these means, a fresh meal for the crew was often obtained; for they not only had fish on board but some would have grapes, whilst others would have fowls and eggs, and our captain was always anxious to get fresh provisions for the ship's company (162)."

A blockade threatened
Now and again, there were even clashes with the enemy: "Whilst on the lookout, we happened to discover the enemy one morning loose their sails, and this we thought was merely to dry them, but it turned out to be otherwise. A Russian fleet of nine sail of the line had just come down the Gut of Gibraltar, and wanted to enter

Cadiz harbour. We were now in a somewhat awkward predicament, not being certain whether that nation had declared war with England or not. But at all events we prepared for action. Our admiral sent his boat with an officer to the Russian admiral to inform him that he could not go in, and, if he attempted, that we must dispute the point with him. Our force being nine sail of the line made us but equal, yet we were in an awkward position, for on the other side of us were ten or eleven sail of French and Spanish ships of the line, ready to come out, and no doubt would give their assistance to cripple us. The Russians, however, shaped their course to Lisbon, where I believe they were afterwards captured by one of our squadrons (163)."

From Cadiz, Jack sailed in the *Revenge* to join the Channel squadron, which was blockading Brest: "Our captain having left us, we were joined by another, and the ship put to sea, and we soon found we had become 'Channel gropers', a term given to the Channel fleet in wartime, which is destined to hover about Brest when the wind is fair, for the French fleet to come out, as we were blockading this; and when the wind blows strong into the harbour, so that they could not well get out. In those cases our fleet would sometimes put in at Cawsand or Torbay, and might be what sailors call a fresh beef station. But it is such as few seamen like, for they say it is neither being abroad nor at home.

"One reason why they have a dislike of it is that they are open to the ridicule of seamen who may be coming from foreign stations, as well as by the girls and people in the sea-port towns, by cantingly telling them they would never have the scurvy, or that they might as well be by their mother's fireside and tied to the apron-strings, as merely running in and out of harbour. And nothing hurts Jack's feelings more than being taunted of anything unmanly or inferior (164)."

The funeral of Lord Nelson took place in London on Thursday, 9th January, 1806. His body had been brought back preserved in a barrel of brandy. *The Times* reported: "Yesterday the burial of this illustrious warrior took place in St. Paul's Cathedral. An hour before daylight the drums of the different volunteer corps in every part of the metropolis beat to arms. The summons was quickly obeyed, and soon after these troops lined the streets in two ranks

"Channel gropers"

Nelson's funeral

Funeral procession of Lord Nelson arrives at St. Paul's Cathedral, London

from St. Paul's Churchyard to the Admiralty. The Life Guards, too, were mounted at their post in Hyde Park at daybreak, when the carriages of the nobility, &c., with the mourning coaches appointed to form part of the procession, began to assemble at eight o'clock, in a line from Hyde Park Corner to Cumberland Gate. By ten, about 106 carriages were assembled, of which number near 60 were mourning coaches, principally filled with naval officers, all of which under the direction of the proper officers, were marshalled in their due order of precedence, and proceeded into St. James's Park, to be in readiness to fall into the procession, on the proper signal.

"In St. James's Park were drawn up all the regiments of cavalry and infantry quartered within 100 miles of London, who had served in the glorious campaigns in Egypt, after the memorable victory at the Nile; and a detachment of flying artillery, with twelve field pieces, and their ammunition tumbrils. At half-past ten, the procession commenced from the Admiralty, with the march of the several regiments, led by his Royal Highness the Duke of York, attended by his aides-de-camp and staff . . . (165)"

The Times said of Nelson: "In tracing this illustrious mariner from the ardour of his boyish days to the active magnanimity with which he closed his glorious life, the mind must be dazzled with the brilliant variety of his action in every part of it.

A tribute to Nelson

"What dangers has he not encountered? What hardships has he not suffered? What obstacles has he not subdued? What seas has he not sailed, what service has he not performed? What duty has he left undone? . . . The nation, alas! now weaves the cypress with the laurel; and, while she prepares her eulogy, the tear glistens in the eye of glory (166)."

EXTRACT FROM THE SIGNALS OF THE FRIGATE *Euryalus*

October 19th

TIME	SIGNAL	MESSAGE
6.04 a.m.	*Sirius* to *Euryalus*	Enemy have their topsail yards hoisted.
7.00 a.m.	*Sirius* to *Euryalus*	Enemy's ships are coming out of port.
7.10 a.m.	*Euryalus* to *General*	Close nearer the Admiral.
7.20 a.m.	*Euryalus* to *Weasel* and *Pickle*	Come within hail (shouting distance)
7.20 a.m.	*Euryalus* to *Phoebe*	Repeat signals between the Admiral and lookout ships west.
7.20 a.m.	*Euryalus* to *Phoebe*	Enemy are coming out of port.
7.30 a.m.	*Euryalus* to *Phoebe* and *Weasel*	Come within hail (shouting distance)
8.40 a.m.	*Euryalus* to *Weasel*	Permission is given to part company.
8.40 a.m.	*Euryalus* to *Weasel*	Make all possible sail with safety to the masts.
8.40 a.m.	*Euryalus* to *Weasel*	Let one reef out of topsails.
10.20 a.m.	*Naiad* to *Euryalus*	Ships ahead repeated Mediterranean signals.
11.05 a.m.	*Euryalus* to *Naiad*	Nineteen under sail—all the rest topyards hoisted except rear. Admiral and one line of battle ship.
11.05 a.m.	*Euryalus* to *Naiad*	Little wind in harbour. Two enemy ships at anchor.
12.00 a.m.	*Euryalus* to *Naiad*	Notwithstanding little wind, many of enemy persevere to get outward, the rest except one line ready yards hoisted.
1.50 p.m.	*Euryalus* to *Naiad*	Wind at present west. Enemy persevering to work outward. Seven of line already outside, and two frigates.
2.30 p.m.	*Euryalus* to *Sirius*	Close nearer Admiral.
3.20 p.m.	*Euryalus* to *Naiad*	See the Admiral or (make sure you) know his position.
3.40 p.m.	*Euryalus* to *Sirius*	Close nearer Admiral.
4.00 p.m.	*Euryalus* to *Sirius*	Repeat your last signal.

TIME	SIGNAL	MESSAGE
6.00 a.m.	*Euryalus* to *Naiad*	Repeat signals between Admiral and lookout ships.
8.30 a.m.	*Euryalus* to *Agamemnon*	Enemy in sight to north-east.
8.55 a.m.	*Euryalus* to *Agamemnon*	Ships are seen on the larboard tack by the wind.
9.10 a.m.	*Euryalus* to *Agamemnon*	There have been thirteen ships outside port, the rest with yards hoisted. Enemy cannot see English fleet. All the rest coming out with expedition (speed).
1.50 p.m.	*Euryalus* to *Sirius*	Leave off chase.
1.55 p.m.	*Sirius* to *Euryalus*	Enemy in sight.
2.00 p.m.	*Euryalus* to *Sirius*	Keep enemy in sight.
2.10 p.m.	*Euryalus* to *Sirius*	Enemy in sight. Engage the enemy on the starboard side – or weather side if on a wind.
4.20 p.m.	*Euryalus* to *Naiad* and *Phoebe*	Close nearer Admiral
5.10 p.m.	*Euryalus* to *Naiad* and *Phoebe*	Make sail from the fleet and look out in direction pointed out.
5.25 p.m.	*Euryalus* to *Naiad* and *Phoebe*	Close near Admiral.

October 21st
The day of Trafalgar

TIME	SIGNAL	MESSAGE
7.00 a.m.	*Victory* to *General* via *Euryalus*	Prepare for battle. Bear up and steer east.
Noon	*Victory* to *Euryalus*	Prepare to anchor.
12.20 p.m.	*Victory* to *General* via *Euryalus*	Engage the enemy more closely.

October 22nd
Mopping up the enemy

TIME	SIGNAL	MESSAGE
10.30 a.m.	*Euryalus* to *Sirius*	Leave off chase.
11.10 a.m.	*Euryalus* to *Polyphemus*	Pass within hail.
11.35 a.m.	*Euryalus* to *Achille*	Stay by prizes.
11.54 a.m.	*Euryalus* to *General*	Close nearer ship indicated.
Noon	*Melpomene* to *Euryalus*	Permission to make more sail?
1.30 p.m.	*Euryalus* to *Minotaur*	Cross topgallant yards.

October 23rd

TIME	SIGNAL	MESSAGE
11.30 a.m.	*Euryalus* to *General*	Leave of chase southwest.
11.45 a.m.	Several ships to *Euryalus*	Enemy are coming out of port.
11.50 a.m.	*Téméraire* to *Euryalus*	We are in distress and obliged to part company, and require another ship to see this one into port.
12.00 a.m.	*Euryalus* to *General*	Prepare for battle, and for anchoring, with springs on the cables and the end of the sheet cable taken in at the stern port.
2.44 p.m.	*Euryalus* to *Britannia*	Send the number of men indicated on board captured ship.
3.08 p.m.	*Euryalus* to *Britannia*	Make all possible sail with safety to the masts.

Table of Dates

1759 Birth of Horatio Nelson.

1776 Nelson commissioned as 2nd lieutenant of a frigate.

1779 Nelson appointed to his first captaincy (the frigate *Hinching-brooke*).

1782 Admiral Rodney wins great naval victory over the French navy of Louis XVI.

1789 The French Revolution begins.

1793 England at war with France.

1794 The Glorious First of June: Admiral Howe destroys French convoy fleet.

1797 England wins naval victory over Spain at Cape St. Vincent (14th February).

1798 Nelson wins the Battle of the Nile over the French fleet.

1799 Britain forms Second Coalition against France, with aid of Austria, Russia and Turkey.

1800 Collapse of the Second Coalition.

1801 Nelson wins great victory over the French fleet at Copenhagen, and destroys Napoleon's planned blockade of Britain.

1802 Peace of Amiens: short peace between England and France.

1803 Britain and France at war again.
Nelson appointed C-in-C Mediterranean, with flagship *Victory*.

1804 Napoleon crowns himself Emperor of France.

1805 Great English naval victory at Trafalgar off the coast of Portugal (21st October). Death of Nelson in action.

1806 Nelson receives state funeral (9th January) in St. Paul's Cathedral, London.

1815 The French wars end with the defeat of Napoleon at Waterloo.

1833 Press gangs formally abolished although none had been used since 1815.

1843 Nelson's Column erected in Trafalgar Square, London.

A Nautical Glossary

BEAM A ship's greatest width.

BLOCKADE To block every approach to a port or country.

BRIG A two-masted, square-rigged vessel.

BROADSIDE The firing at the same time of all the guns on a ship's side.

BULKHEAD Partition below decks.

CARRONADE A heavy cannon devastating at short range.

CAT-O'-NINE-TAILS Rope whip with nine knotted lashes.

COMMISSION Royal order appointing an officer, or ordering a ship to prepare for voyage ("putting a ship into commission").

COXSWAIN Seaman in charge of a ship's boat, such as a longboat.

CROSS TREES Horizontal spars fixed to ship's masts.

DOG WATCH A half watch of two hours.

FIGUREHEAD Carved lifelike figure fixed to the bows of a sailing ship.

FLAGSHIP A ship carrying an admiral, and flying his flag.

FORECASTLE A short raised deck built on a ship's bows.

FRIGATE A vessel smaller and faster than a battleship, often used for sighting, and carrying messages.

FUSILLADE The firing of shot all at once, or without a pause.

GRAPE SHOT A number of pieces of small shot fired loose.

GROG Rum mixed with water.

GUN PORTS Trap doors in a ship's sides out of which the cannon fired.

HOLYSTONE Nickname for sandstone used for scrubbing decks.

JURY MAST A temporary mast, e.g. fitted during a storm or battle.

LARBOARD Port-side or left side of a ship facing ahead.

LEAGUE Naval measure of distance, about three miles.

LOBLOLLY MEN A surgeon's sickbay attendants.

MAGAZINE Store for gunpowder.

MIDSHIPMAN Naval officer of lowest rank.

POOP The highest deck on a ship (a stern deck).

POWDER MONKEY Boy detailed to keep a gun supplied with gunpowder.

PRIVATEER Privately owned vessel allowed to plunder enemy ships.

PURSER Ship's officer in charge of provisions.

QUARTER DECK Raised deck on the stern of a ship reserved for officers, immediately below the poop deck.

SCURVY Disease characterized by swollen gums, spots and fatigue and caused by lack of vitamin C.

SHEET A rope used to hold and control the sails.

SHROUDS Ropes fixed to the ship's sides to support the mast.

SQUADRON Part of a fleet.

STARBOARD Right side of a ship, facing ahead.

TACK To make headway against the wind by changing course frequently from side to side.

WARDROOM Officers' recreation and dining room aboard ship.

WEEVIL Kind of beetle often found in ship's biscuits.

List of Sources

(1) Sir Charles Middleton, memorandum quoted in Navy Records Society, XXXIX, p. 24

(2) H. W. Hodges & E. A. Hughes, *Select Naval Documents*, p. 203

(3) *Ibid*

(4) Admiral Collingwood, letter to J. E. Blackett, 9th August, 1803, *Select Naval Documents* p. 209

(5) Sir Edward Pellew, Parliamentary Debates, 15th March, 1804. Quoted *Select Naval Documents*, p. 210

(6) Letter of Napoleon to Admiral Ganteaume, 6th September, 1804 (*Navy Records Society* XXI, p. 59)

(7) *Ibid*

(8) Collingwood, letter to Blackett, 4th February, 1805, *S.N.D.*, p. 212

(9) Admiral Nelson to Alexander Davison, 12th December, 1803 (*Nelson's Letters*, Everyman edition)

(10) *Memoirs of John Nicol*, ed. Alexander Laing (Cassell, 1937)

(11) Captain Whitby to Cornwallis, 11th June, 1804 (Navy Record Society, XIV, 343)

(12) *Ibid*

(13) *Nelson's Letters*

(14) Quoted in *England Expects*, Dudley Pope.

(15) *Ibid*

(16) Sermon of Dr. Watson, Bishop of Landaff; quoted in *England Expects*, 55

(17) Quoted *England Expects*, p. 55

(18) *Select Naval Documents*, 216

(19) Jack Nastyface, *Nautical Economy* (1836)

(20) *Memoirs of John Nicol, ibid*

(21) Captains' Letters in the Public Record Office; Captain J. C. Searle, 26th April, 1803

(22) Jack Nastyface, *ibid*

(23) Quoted *England Expects*, p. 71

(24) *Ibid*

(25) *Select Naval Documents*, p. 203

(26) *Ibid*, p. 200

(27) Jack Nastyface, *ibid*

(28) *Memoirs of George Watson*; quoted in *From the Lower Deck*, Henry Baynham (1969)

(29) Jack Nastyface, *supra*

(30) Manuscript memoirs of Samuel Stokes, quoted in *From the Lower Deck*

(31) *Memoirs of Samuel Leech* (1843); quoted in *From the Lower Deck*

(32) *Memoirs of John Nicol, supra*

(33) *Memoirs of George Watson, supra*

(34) Jack Nastyface, *supra*

(35) John Masefield, *Sea Life in Nelson's Time*, (Methuen, 1905)

(36) *Ibid*

(37) Jack Nastyface, *supra*

(38) *Ibid*

(39) *Ibid*

(40) *Ibid*

(41) *Memoirs of Samuel Leech, supra*

(42) *Memoirs of John Nicol, supra*

(43) Jack Nastyface, *supra*

(44) *Ibid*

(45) *Ibid*

(46) *Ibid*

(47) *Ibid*

(48) *Ibid*

(49) *Ibid*

(50) *Ibid*

(51) *Ibid*

(52) *Memoirs of George Watson, supra*

(53) Jack Nastyface, *supra*

(54) Letter of Villeneuve to Decrès; quoted *England Expects*, p. 86

(55) *Nelson's Letters, supra*

(56) *Ibid*

(57) *Ibid*

(58) *Ibid*

(59) *Ibid*

(60) *Ibid*; 31st August, 1805

(61) *Ibid*; 4th September, 1805

(62) *Ibid*

(63) *Ibid*

(64) *Ibid*; Admiralty, 7th September, 1805

(65) *Ibid*

(66) *Ibid*

(67) Log of the *Victory*, 14th September, 1805

(68) *Nelson's Letters*, 14th September, 1805

(69) *Ibid*

(70) *Ibid*, 25th September, 1805

(71) *Ibid*

(72) *Ibid*, 27th September, 1805, off Cape St. Vincent

(73) *Ibid*, 30th September, 1805

(74) *Ibid*, 1st October, 1805

(75) *Ibid*, 4th October, 1805

(76) *Ibid*, 5th October, 1805

(77) *Ibid*, 10th October, 1805

(78) *Ibid*, 9th October, 1805

(79) *Ibid*, 9th October, 1805

(80) Letter of Lt. George L. Browne, from the *Victory* at Spithead, 4th December, 1805

(81) Jack Nastyface, *supra*

(82) *Nelson's Letters*, 19th October, 1805

(83) *Ibid*, 20th October, 1805

(84) *Ibid*, 20th October, 1805

(85) Quoted Ian Ribbons, *Monday 21st October* (O.U.P.)

(86) *Ibid*

(87) *Ibid*

(88) *Narrative of the Death of Lord Nelson*, Dr. William Beatty

(89) Quoted Ribbons, *supra*

(90) Jack Nastyface, *supra*

(91) Ribbons, *supra*

(92) *Nelson's Letters*, 21st October, 1805

(93) Codicil to Lord Nelson's will, *Nelson's Letters*

(94) Jack Nastyface, *supra*

(95) *Ibid*

(96) *Ibid*

(97) Letter of Capt. Robert Moorsom to his father Richard Moorsom, 1st November, 1805

(98) Letter of Lt. George L.

(99) *Ibid*

(100) Quoted Ribbons, *supra*

(101) Jack Nastyface, *supra*

(102) *Ibid*

(103) *Ibid*

(104) *Death of Lord Nelson*, Beatty, *supra*

(105) *Quoted Ribbons*

(106) *Ibid*

(107) *Ibid*

(108) *Ibid*

(109) *Ibid*

(110) *Ibid*

(111) *Ibid*

(112) *Ibid*

(113) *Ibid*

(114) *Ibid*

(115) *Collingwood's Despatches*, in *Letters and Despatches of Lord Nelson*, ed. Sir H. Nicholas, vol. 7 (London, 1846)

(116) Jack Nastyface, *supra*

(117) Quoted in *England Expects*

(118) *Ibid*

(119) Quoted by Ribbons

(120) Quoted in *England Expects*

(121) *Death of Nelson*, Beatty

(122) Quoted in *England Expects*

(123) *Ibid*

(124) *Ibid*

(125) *Ibid*

(126) Quoted Ribbons

(127) *Ibid*

(128) *Ibid*

(129) Log of the *Belleisle*

(130) Quoted in *England Expects*

(131) *Ibid*

(132) *Ibid*

(133) *Ibid*

(134) *Ibid*

(135) *Death of Nelson*, Beatty

(136) Jack Nastyface, *supra* Browne, *supra*

(137) *Ibid*

(138) *Letters of the English Seaman*. "Lt. Paul Nicholas," E. Hallam Moorhouse, 1910

(139) Log of the *Euryalus*, Captain Blackwood

(140) Log of the *Prince*. *Great Sea Fights*, Navy Records Society, Vol. 2

(141) Jack Nastyface, *supra*

(142) *Ibid*

(143) *Ibid*

(144) *Ibid*

(145) Quoted Ribbons

(146) *Ibid*

(147) *Ibid*

(148) Letter to Richard Moorsom, his father, 1st December, 1805

(149) Log of the *Belleisle*, *Great Sea Fights*, Navy Records Society, vol. 2

(150) Log of the *Prince*, *ibid*

(151) Quoted Ribbons

(152) Jack Nastyface, *supra*

(153) *Ibid*

(154) Lady Bessborough to Lord Granville Leveson-Gower, quoted in *England Expects*, p. 39

(155) Quoted *England Expects*, p. 39

(156) *Ibid*

(157) *The Naval Chronicle*

(158) Lady Elizabeth Harvey to her son in the United States

(159) *John Nicol Memoirs*, *supra*

(160) Quoted in *From the Lower Deck*, p. 2

(161) Jack Nastyface, *supra*

(162) *Ibid*

(163) *Ibid*

(164) *Ibid*

(165) Obituary in *The Times*, 10th January, 1806

(166) *Ibid*

Picture Credits

The Publishers wish to thank the following for their kind permission to reproduce copyright illustrations on the pages mentioned: Trustees of the National Maritime Museum, *jacket,* 10, 31, 35, 36, 41, 42, 45, 49 (right), 82–83, 96; the Mansell Collection, *frontispiece,* 13, 17, 22, 25, 27, 31 (right), 32 (left and right), 37, 40, 44, 49 (left), 51, 52, 55, 64, 76–77, 80, 84, 86–87, 100–101, 106, 109, 112; the Radio Times Hulton Picture Library, 20, 30, 31 (left and centre), 38, 39, 43, 56, 65, 73, 90–91, 97. Other illustrations appearing in this book are the property of the Wayland Picture Library.

Further Reading

The following is a list of some of the most important books necessary for a serious study of the years of Trafalgar. Most offer material which is not only well documented, but very readable.

Nelson's Letters, ed. Geoffrey Rawson (Everyman Library, 244).
The Life of Nelson, A. T. Mahan (1897).
The Influence of Seapower upon History 1660–1783, A. T. Mahan (1890).
Trafalgar, Edouard Desbriere (Paris, 1907).
Great Sea Fights 1794–1805, ed. T. Sturges Jackson (Navy Record Society, 1900).
Fighting Instructions 1530–1816, ed. J. S. Corbett (Navy Records Society, 1905).
Select Naval Documents, ed. H. W. Hodges & E. A. Hughes (1922).
England Expects, Dudley Pope (1959).
Medicine and the Navy, J. J. Keevil, 3 vols. (1957).
From the Lower Deck, Henry Baynham (1969).
Sea Life in Nelson's Time, John Masefield (1905).
Letters of the English Seamen, E. Hallam Moorehouse (1910).
The Years of Victory, Sir Arthur Bryant (1945).

Index

127